Adobe Acrobat® in One Hour
FOR LAWYERS

ERNIE SVENSON

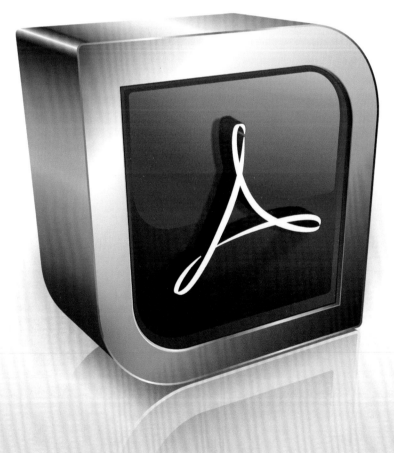

**ABALAW
PRACTICE
DIVISION**
The Business of Practicing Law

Commitment to Quality: The Law Practice Division is committed to quality in our publications. Our authors are experienced practitioners in their fields. Prior to publication, the contents of all our books are rigorously reviewed by experts to ensure the highest quality product and presentation. Because we are committed to serving our readers' needs, we welcome your feedback on how we can improve future editions of this book.

Cover design by RIPE Creative, Inc.

Screenshots and information about Adobe Acrobat® are not to be taken as an endorsement of this book by Adobe Systems Incorporated. Adobe® reserves all rights to the use of images related to its software, and the use of those images in this book is reprinted with permission from Adobe Systems Incorporated. Adobe® and Adobe Acrobat® are registered trademarks, and all rights in those marks are reserved.

Nothing contained in this book is to be considered as the rendering of legal advice for specific cases, and readers are responsible for obtaining such advice from their own legal counsel. This book and any forms and agreements herein are intended for educational and informational purposes only.

The products and services mentioned in this publication are under or may be under trademark or service mark protection. Product and service names and terms are used throughout only in an editorial fashion, to the benefit of the product manufacturer or service provider, with no intention of infringement. Use of a product or service name or term in this publication should not be regarded as affecting the validity of any trademark or service mark.

The Law Practice Division of the American Bar Association offers an educational program for lawyers in practice. Books and other materials are published in furtherance of that program. Authors and editors of publications may express their own legal interpretations and opinions, which are not necessarily those of either the American Bar Association or the Law Practice Division unless adopted pursuant to the bylaws of the Association. The opinions expressed do not reflect in any way a position of the Division or the American Bar Association.

Printed in the United States of America

17 16 15 14 13   5 4 3 2 1

Library of Congress Cataloging-in-Publication Data

Svenson, Ernie.
   Adobe acrobat in one hour for lawyers / by Ernie Svenson.
      pages cm
   Includes bibliographical references and indexes.
   ISBN 978-1-62722-216-7
  1. Practice of law—United States—Automation. 2. Adobe Acrobat. 3. File conversion (Computer science)
  4. Portable document software. I. Title.
   KF322.S84   2013
   005.7'26—dc23
                                                                                    2013038966

Discounts are available for books ordered in bulk. Special consideration is given to state bars, CLE programs, and other bar-related organizations. Inquire at Book Publishing, American Bar Association, 321 N. Clark Street, Chicago, Illinois 60654.

www.ShopABA.org

Contents

Acknowledgments

Thanks to Tom Mighell for proposing the book, and to Denise Constantine, Lindsay Dawson, and Laura Bolesta of the American Bar Association, and to Jeff Flax, for managing the production, and providing expert guidance. Thanks to Lenore Howard for her exceptional copy-editing; she rocks!

Special thanks go to the peer reviewers of early drafts of the book: David Masters, Rick Borstein, Catherine Sanders-Reach, Aaron Krigelski, Dane Ciolino, Casey Flaherty, Judge David Nuffer, Andrew Legrand, Kris Canaday, and my extremely tech-savvy wife, Rebecca Diamante.

Most of all, thanks to the readers of my PDF for Lawyers blog; their interest (and excellent questions) pushed me to learn more about PDFs, and discover many amazing PDF tricks and tips.

About the Author

Ernie Svenson has practiced commercial litigation for twenty-six years, first with a mid-sized New Orleans law firm, and then for seven years as a solo practitioner. He's now a full-time speaker on tech-related topics.

In 2004, Ernie started a blog called PDFforLawyers .com, geared toward helping lawyers learn to make better use of PDF files in their practice. He later co-founded PaperlessChase.com to help busy attorneys become more organized by learning to practice law without being bogged down by paper.

He's also the author of another ABA LPM book, *Blogging in One Hour for Lawyers*. To find out more about him, just Google "ernie attorney," or follow him on Twitter: @ernieattorney.

Introduction

Who Will Benefit from This Book

This book can be used by lawyers, legal professionals, law students, or anyone who wants to become more proficient working with PDFs using Adobe Acrobat software.

Editions and Versions of Acrobat Covered

This book covers editions X and XI of Acrobat (earlier editions of Acrobat are no longer supported by Adobe). The interface of edition X is pretty much the same as edition XI, with one important difference, as shown in the two screenshots in Figure i:

Figure i Acrobat X Interface

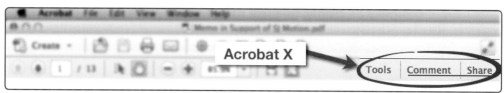

In edition X, the **Task Pane** contains a **Share** menu, which allows quick access to Adobe's SendNow service (no longer promoted in Acrobat XI).

Figure ii Acrobat XI Interface

In edition XI of Acrobat, the **Comment** menu was moved to the right, and the **Sign** menu now appears, signaling Adobe's decision to promote the use of electronic signatures.

Both Acrobat X and Acrobat XI come in two versions, at least for Windows users. This book will also address key aspects of both the **Standard** and **Professional** versions of Acrobat for Windows, as well as the Professional version for Mac (there is no Standard version for the Mac).

The Agenda

Overview. Get an overview of PDFs, and why lawyers should learn more about how to work with them.

Part I: Basic Skills

Section 1: Setting Preferences. Discover how to create the ideal work environment in Acrobat.

Section 2: Viewing PDFs. Learn to quickly rotate, zoom, and see things with an optimal view.

Section 3: Navigating PDFs. Find out how to move around in a PDF quickly, without fumbling.

Section 4: Interface: Menus and Toolbars. Understand the overall layout and where to find the tools you'll work with most often.

Section 5: Creating PDFs. Find out how to turn any file (or set of files) into a PDF.

Section 6: Examining PDFs. Learn to troubleshoot problem PDFs, and determine if security has been applied to limit a PDF's access or functionality.

Section 7: Working with Pages. Discover how to rearrange pages in a PDF, remove them, insert new ones, or extract them.

Part II: Intermediate Skills

Section 8: Bookmarks. Learn to quickly set bookmarks and use them to jump to a saved view; in short: discover why they're crucial.

Section 9: Comments. Find out why comments in PDFs are much more powerful than marginalia on paper.

Section 10: Text Editing. Become adept at adding text to a PDF, or changing text that's already there.

Section 11: OCR or "Recognize Text." Discover how to take a PDF that isn't searchable and easily turn it into a searchable PDF.

Section 12: Stamps. Find out how to stamp "Draft" or "Confidential" on a PDF's pages, how to add Exhibit stamps, and how to create signature stamps.

Section 13: Digital Signatures. Discover why true digital signatures are unnecessary, and more trouble than they're worth.

Section 14: Bates Numbering. Learn to append text or sequential numbers to documents you have to produce or manage.

Section 15: Redaction. Find out how to obscure sensitive or confidential text in PDFs.

Section 16: Metadata Removal. Learn to efficiently sanitize hidden data you don't want other people to see.

Section 17: Find and Advanced Search. Become proficient searching for text or phrases inside a single PDF, a group of PDFs, or non-PDF documents.

Section 18: Security. Learn how to apply security to a PDF or group of PDFs to restrict who can open the file and what can be done with it

Section 19: PDF/A. Find out how to create a PDF/A file, which will eventually be the filing standard in all federal courts.

Appendix

Recommended Preference Settings

Keyboard Shortcut Cheat Sheet

Single-Key Accelerator Cheat Sheet

Acrobat Pro v. Standard Checklist

Adobe Reader: Features and Limitations

PDF Workflows in the Law Office

Overview

PDFs have been around for over twenty years. At first, PDFs were a novelty, but now most people are used to opening and reading PDFs. Still, many people get confused about how to work with PDFs, and why they need a program like Acrobat to manipulate PDFs. This book will explain why Acrobat is essential for the modern lawyer, and how legal professionals can use it most effectively.

About PDFs

The term "PDF" is an acronym that stands for "portable document format," a format that was created by Adobe Systems, Incorporated. Think of PDFs as a form of "digital paper"—that is, a way to display text and graphics on a computer or mobile device. The PDF format preserves all of a document's fonts, formatting, colors, and graphics, regardless of what kind of device was used to create the original document.

But PDFs can do more than just display text. For example, they can contain embedded files, and even display multimedia content such as audio and video files. PDF files can also be secured to prevent unauthorized changes or printing, or to limit access to confidential information.

PDFs are increasingly being adopted by state courts for e-filing. It's now mandatory in every federal court; the "original document" filed in the record is nothing more than a bunch of ones and zeros—i.e., a PDF file.

Although PDFs were not created specifically for the legal profession, with the adoption of PDFs as a way of producing case documents, as well as their use in e-filing, lawyers now routinely encounter PDFs as part of their daily practice. It's safe to say that PDFs are now a mainstay in the legal profession. So, it makes sense for lawyers and legal professionals to learn more about how to use PDFs: how to search for a key word or phrase in PDFs, how to tag pages within them, how to create comments, how to Bates stamp and redact sensitive information. And that's exactly what this book is designed to help you learn.

The first step is to understand that not all PDFs are created equal.

Two Types of PDFs

There are two types of PDFs: some have selectable (and searchable) text, and the other kind does not. "Text PDFs" (also called "text-based PDFs") contain selectable and searchable text. "Image PDFs" do not allow text to be selected or searched.

The difference is usually determined by how the PDF was created. Text PDFs are created by a computer that converts, say, a Word or Excel file into a PDF. Image PDFs are created using a scanner (e.g., scanning paper to PDF). Text PDFs are preferable, for a couple of reasons.

- They're searchable, which is always a good thing.
- The text can be selected and copied and pasted elsewhere, which is handy.
- The text is often easier to read than image PDFs.
- Their file size is smaller, so it takes up less space on your hard drive.

If you have an image PDF, you can use Acrobat to convert it to a text PDF, a process that will be explained in detail in Section 11. For now, just know that text PDFs are better, especially for case documents or any kind of file that you'll want to be able to search or copy text from.

Adobe Reader

Adobe makes a free program called Adobe Reader, which is not as powerful as Adobe Acrobat. Yet, if you ask most people who have the Reader program if they have "Acrobat," they'll answer yes. People seem to think the terms "Reader" and "Acrobat" are interchangeable. They're not.

Adobe Reader is more ubiquitous because it's free. Anyone can easily obtain a copy of it by simply searching online using the phrase "free adobe reader." The latest edition, as of the time of this writing, is edition XI, and although it's not nearly as powerful as Acrobat, it's quite useful for several basic tasks, such as navigating a PDF or searching its contents. Mostly, Adobe makes it available for free so people can easily open and view PDFs.

Edition XI of Reader also allows you to create comments of the type covered in Section 9. However, it doesn't allow for the kind of basic PDF manipulation most legal professionals will need to do: bookmarking pages, rearranging pages, Bates stamping or redacting. Let's be clear: you need Adobe Acrobat if you're serious about using PDFs in your law practice.

Why Use Adobe Acrobat?

Adobe Acrobat is not the only software that allows lawyers to manipulate PDFs, but it's widely used and very powerful. So, if you're *not* going to use it you should have a good reason. Yes, it's expensive. But if you use a cheaper program, it may not do all of the things you'll want to do; and if you opt for another program, you're less likely to get help figuring out how to use it effectively in your practice. Also, most of the helpful plug-ins for lawyers, such as specialized exhibit stickers, only work with Acrobat (usually only with the Windows version). If you aren't going to use Acrobat, make sure you understand exactly what options you're giving up. Odds are you're giving up more than you want to.

Standard v. Professional

Each edition of Acrobat (X or XI) comes in two versions: Acrobat Standard and Acrobat Professional, unless you are a Mac user, in which case you can only buy Acrobat Professional.

If you're buying your first copy of Acrobat, you should buy the Professional version first. It has two important features that every law firm will need from time to time: (1) Bates stamping, and (2) redaction. There are other benefits to having the Pro version of Acrobat, but those two are the key reasons why every law firm needs at least one copy of Acrobat Professional.

If your law firm has several lawyers or legal professionals, you might want to save money (approximately $60–$100) and buy mostly Acrobat Standard. However, if you are using Mac computers, there is no choice: you have to buy the Professional version.

Adobe has an online comparison chart showing the differences between Acrobat XI, XI Standard, and XI Professional. Here's a short link to that online page: http://is.gd/Q83sxg.

Free Trial of Acrobat

Adobe offers free trial versions of most of its software, which can be downloaded from its website. Acrobat Professional is among the programs that you can try for a short time (typically thirty days) for free. The trial version is fully functional and offers every feature of the paid version.

The URL for the free download is: http://www.adobe.com/downloads.

Mac v. PC: Some Differences

PDFs created with Acrobat (or any other third-party PDF creation program) will look exactly the same no matter what kind of computer you use. However, there are some differences between Acrobat for Macs and Acrobat for PCs, besides the fact that Mac users have to buy the Professional version.

The interfaces of the Mac and PC programs are slightly different, but for the most part the differences aren't noticeable. In fact, anyone who uses the Mac program will be completely adept with the PC program (and vice-versa). I use both programs and never get confused, because the interfaces are almost exactly the same. (However, because I mainly use a Mac, most of the screenshots in the book will show the Mac program.)

Keyboard Shortcuts Are Important

To get the most out of any software, it behooves you to learn the commonly used keyboard shortcuts. The most important ones for Acrobat are set forth in the Appendix.

The keyboard shortcuts are the same on a Mac or PC, with one variant. On a Mac, the modifier key is typically the **Command** key, while on a PC it is the **Control** key. So, when I describe a keyboard shortcut, such as the one for creating bookmarks, I'll say, "You should use **CMD/CTRL + B**." The text string **CMD/CTRL** means that on a Mac you'd use the **Command** key, and on a PC you'd use the **Control** key.

Figure 0.1 Keyboard Shortcut Modifier Keys (PC vs. Mac)

As a mnemonic, remember that keyboard shortcuts are all about command and control. Macs are easy to train, so you can *command* a Mac. PCs are more complex, so you have to learn to *control* them. You might want to come up with your own way of remembering which key modifier applies to your computer operating system.

For a comprehensive list of Acrobat XI's keyboard commands, go to the **Help** menu and choose **Adobe Acrobat XI Help**. On a Mac, you can easily find the shortcuts list from there. On a PC, find the heading that says **Workspace** and then look for **Keyboard Shortcuts**.

How to Learn from This Book

Let's be realistic: you won't learn everything that's covered in this book in one hour. But you can quickly get a sense of some practical ways you can use Acrobat to improve your law practice. Most likely, the book will serve as a frequently consulted reference manual.

The way to learn Acrobat is to focus on one skill at a time, beginning with the skills you're likely to use most often; for example, changing page views or navigating through a PDF using bookmarks—as opposed to Bates stamping or doing redaction.

Even after you read this book, you'll have to find ways to keep up with Acrobat as Adobe releases new editions, or as new tricks and tips are identified by lawyers who use it. For this, I recommend you visit the following websites related to the use of PDFs in the practice of law:

- **Acrobat for Legal Professionals** (http://blogs.adobe.com/acrolaw/) A site created by Rick Borstein, who works for Adobe and knows a lot about using Acrobat in general. He isn't a lawyer, but his blog focuses on the legal profession, and has a trove of useful information for lawyers and legal professionals. Definitely subscribe to his e-mail newsletter, so you're assured of getting the latest posts. And check out the category links on the right-hand side of his blog; there are some incredibly useful posts there, organized by topic.

- **PDF for Lawyers** (www.pdfforlawyers.com) A blog I created in 2004 to help lawyers learn how to get more out of PDFs in their law practices. There's an e-mail newsletter that comes out twice a month, so you might want to subscribe to that as well to keep up with new information about using PDFs in the legal profession.

- **Paperless Chase** (http://paperlesschase.com) I started this website (and a company of the same name) to help lawyers get more organized by pushing less paper. Since using PDFs is crucial to being paperless, you'll find a lot of useful information about how to use PDFs there as well.

If you crave up-to-the-minute PDF tips and news, check out the PDF for Lawyers stream on Twitter (www.twitter.com/pdflawyer) or the dedicated Facebook page (www.facebook.com/PDFforLawyers), whichever medium you prefer; the information is the same in both places.

Finally, here's a tip for quickly figuring out how to do something in Acrobat: open your favorite Internet browser and search the web using some variant of this phrase: "How do I [describe action] in Acrobat?" Rick Borstein says that's what he does, and he works for Adobe and knows more about it than anyone I'm acquainted with. That troubleshooting tip will probably work for you as well.

Part I

Basic Skills

The Basic Skills section is about getting properly set up, and then learning the key skills you'll use most of the time when viewing and navigating PDFs.

Setting Preferences

You need to have your Acrobat software set up so you can quickly access tools you use most often. You should also have the interface customized to show tools and views that you prefer. Granted, setting preferences can seem tedious. But it's important if you want things to work smoothly, and to avoid frustration.

1.1 Accessing Preferences

How you access the preferences is slightly different, depending on whether you're using a PC or a Mac. On a PC, select *Edit > Preferences*. On a Mac, select *Adobe > Preferences*. The keyboard shortcut for accessing the preferences on a PC is **CTRL + K**, and on a Mac it's **CMD + ,** (comma).

1.2 The Categories Pane

Once you select the preferences option, the next view is the same, regardless of what kind of computer you use, and unfortunately, the next dialog box presents a bewildering array of options. Fortunately, most of the options you'll want to fiddle with are among the five top left options under the **Categories** list, as Figure 1.1 reveals.

Figure 1.1 Setting Comment Preferences

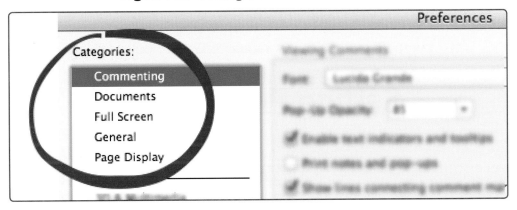

Spend some time clicking on each of five terms circled in red and see what options are available to you.

1.3 Commenting Options

The **Commenting** category has default options that are set the way most lawyers will want to have them, with one exception. Almost every lawyer who uses the highlighter tool (discussed in Section 9.1) will want to have the highlighted text automatically copied into the comment text that goes with it. So, check the box that says **Copy selected text into Highlight, Cross-Out, and Underline comment pop-ups**.

Doing so will cause Acrobat to automatically copy text that you highlight into the comments box. Most of the time you'll want to do this, and it is easy to quickly remove in situations where you want to put in your own text comment.

1.4 Single-Key Accelerators

Under the **General** sidebar, you might want to activate the first option, called **Use single-key accelerators to access tools**, as shown in Figure 1.2.

Figure 1.2

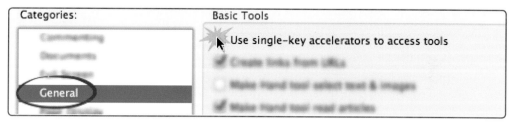

This is something that power-users always enable because it allows them to switch quickly from one tool to another simply by tapping on the key that corresponds to a particular tool. Not all tools can be accessed by the single-key accelerators, but some of the most useful ones can: **Select** text (V), **Highlight** text (U), **Hand** tool (H), **Stamp** tool (K).

Section 2

Viewing PDFs

PDFs can be displayed in a web browser, but most of the time you'll be viewing PDFs in Adobe Acrobat, so we'll focus on viewing PDFs that way.

Acrobat presents you with four main viewing choices: (1) **Rotate View**, (2) **Page Navigation**, (3) **Page Display**, and (4) **Zoom**. The easiest way to remember what these options are is to click on the **View** menu (see Figure 2.1).

Figure 2.1 View Menu Options

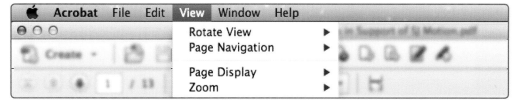

The purpose of each option is mostly self-evident, but it's important to know how they all work and to be able to use them without a lot of fiddling around. We'll cover Page Navigation in Section 3, so for now let's talk about the other three choices.

2.1 Rotation

One of the most common things you'll encounter in dealing with PDFs is a rotation problem. The **View** menu has **Rotate View** as its first option, probably for that very reason (see Figure 2.2). Sometimes it's a whole document that was, for whatever bizarre reason, rotated on its side. Sometimes it's just one or two random pages.

Figure 2.2 Rotate View—Menu Selection

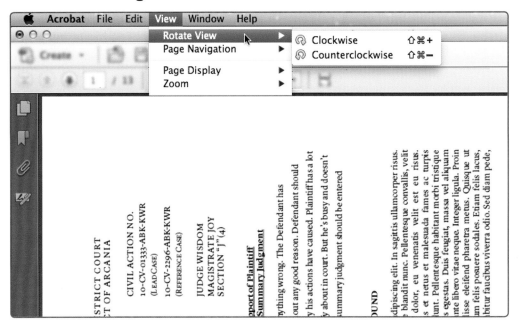

Using Rotate View is great if the entire PDF is not rotated correctly; but this method will *not* let you rotate select pages. Nor will it let you save the rotation change you make. Thus, this option is almost always *totally worthless*.

So, let's talk about the only truly useful rotation method.

For that, you need to move over to the **Task Pane**. From there, select *Tools > Pages > Rotate*, and you'll get a dialog box like the one in Figure 2.3.

Figure 2.3 Rotate View—Task Pane Selection

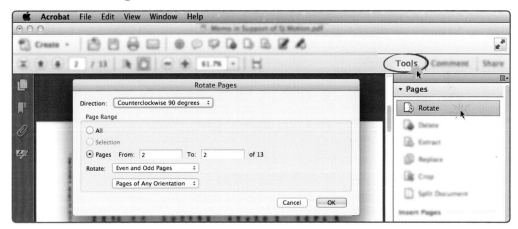

From here, you can choose to rotate one page or a range of pages. You also have the option of rotating the direction as follows: clockwise, counterclockwise, or 180 degrees. Once you've rotated the pages the way you want, choose *Save* from the *File* menu to lock in that preference.

The best way to get to this dialog box is to learn the keyboard shortcut, which is **CMD/CTRL + SHIFT + R**.

2.2 Page Display (Single or Scrolling)

You probably noticed **Page Display** in Figure 1.1, where we discussed setting global preferences for displaying PDFs. You can also control the page display and set preferences at the individual PDF level.

If you want to switch the page display in the current PDF, use the **View** menu commands. Select ***Page Display*** and set it to ***Single Page View*** or, if you prefer, to ***Enable Scrolling*** (see Figure 2.4).

Figure 2.4 Page Display—Menu Selection

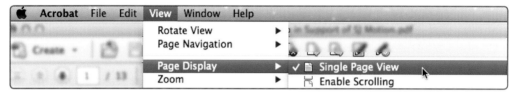

Most lawyers and legal professionals seem to prefer the Single Page View, except when they need to copy text that runs across two pages. When you choose to Enable Scrolling, you can then copy from one page to another; it's the only way to accomplish this.

The default toolbar in Acrobat contains tool icons that allow you to quickly switch between Single Page View and Enable Scrolling view, and that's the fastest way to switch between those options. The toolbar icons are shown in Figure 2.5:

Figure 2.5 Page Display—Toolbar Selection

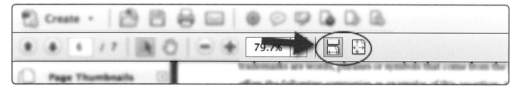

2.3 Zoom: Marquee and Dynamic

Below the Page Display menu option is the very important **Zoom** option. Zoom allows you to view a document page two ways: (1) from top to bottom or from the left to right margins and (2) by zooming in on select regions of the page. Both of these views are useful, but *zooming in* is important to many people, and it's what you tend to think the main purpose of a tool named "Zoom" would be. So, let's focus on that first.

Think about how often you encounter small text in a print document. You know exactly what to do: you either hold the paper closer to your eyes or put on your reading glasses (or maybe you use a magnifying glass). The **Zoom** tool does this for you in a PDF. The point is, you'll use this tool a lot, or you'll quickly get frustrated with viewing PDFs that have small text.

There are several options in how you zoom, and the choices are identified in the menu, as shown in Figure 2.6.

Figure 2.6 Zoom—Menu Options

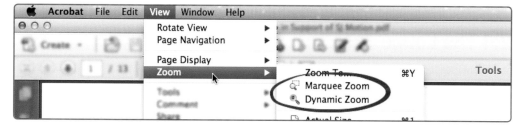

There are two types of zoom: **Marquee Zoom** allows you to select the precise area you want enlarged by clicking and dragging; **Dynamic Zoom** is similar to steadily moving the paper closer to your face. The best way to quickly grasp their respective methods is to use each one. The icons shown in Figure 2.7 give an indication of how each type of zoom works.

Figure 2.7 Zoom Icons: Marquee vs. Dymanic

The Marquee Zoom has the selection graphic, so you know it's the one that lets you zoom by selection. The only way to invoke the Marquee

Zoom is to use the menu. The Dynamic Zoom requires less fiddling to use, and it has a keyboard shortcut that's worth memorizing: **CMD/CTRL + Plus** key or **Minus** key. To keep zooming, just continue pressing the combo for zooming in or zooming out, as desired.

Once you've zoomed in, you might find that you want to move around the page to get to a different area. To do this, hold down the Tab key and drag around as desired. Holding down the space bar gives you the Hand tool, which lets you know that you can drag an area around.

So, here you are, having zoomed in to a microscopic view, and now you want to quickly return to the page view, either **Fit Page** or **Fit Width**. We'll cover this in detail next, but for now just use the key combo **CMD/CTRL + 0** (zero). Or, instead of 0, try 1 and 2 and see what happens. Nice, huh?

2.4 The Loupe Tool

Another way of reading small text is by using the **Loupe** tool, which you can find by selecting *View > Zoom > Loupe Tool*. The tool works by defining an area of focus that is then displayed in zoomed-out view in a separate window, as shown in Figure 2.8.

Figure 2.8 The Loupe Tool

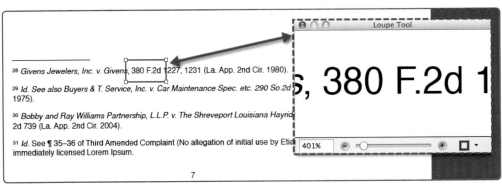

This is not a tool that many legal professionals use often. Mostly it seems to be used by patent lawyers or those who have to examine architectural or engineering documents, which tend to have large dimensions.

2.5 Zoom and Page Display

As we have already discussed, page display involves the layout of the PDF. **Page Display** can be applied to global preferences for Acrobat or to an individual PDF. But you can also override global defaults for any PDF that you are viewing.

As you will recall, the main choices for displaying a page are **Fit Page**, **Fit Width**, **Single Page View**, and **Enable Scrolling**. However, selecting these viewing choices happens in slightly different places on the menu.

First, to change from Single Page View to Enable Scrolling, select *View > Page Display*, and then choose from the options shown in Figure 2.9.

Figure 2.9 Page Display Options

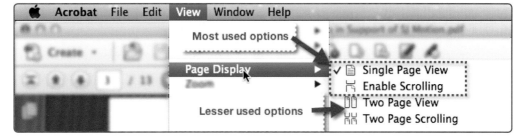

To choose between Fit Page and Fit Width (and even more options), select: *View > Zoom*, and then make additional selections, as indicated in Figure 2.10.

Figure 2.10 Zoom Options

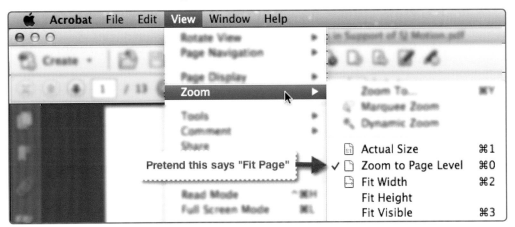

For some reason, Adobe decided not to use "Fit Page" for what is, actually, the Fit Page option. So, pretend that **Zoom to Page Level** says "Fit Page," because that's what it is. More importantly, memorize all of those keyboard shortcuts to switch between the different views quickly.

2.6 Full Screen Mode

Acrobat lets you view PDFs in **Full Screen** mode if you so desire. To invoke this view, select *View > Full Screen Mode*. The keyboard shortcut is **CMD/CTRL + L**. To return to the regular view, press the Escape key.

Using Full Screen view can permit you to display PDFs on a projector in court or in a hearing (similar to a PowerPoint presentation). However, in Full Screen mode the menus disappear, so the only way to zoom in or move around is by using keyboard shortcuts. You can't add comments or draw on the PDF while in Full Screen mode. To advance to the next page while in Full Screen mode, press the right arrow key, and for the previous page, press the left arrow key.

2.7 Split Window Mode

You can split a PDF into two windows, which is sometimes useful for viewing two different sections of a document simultaneously. To split the view, select **Window > Split** (see Figure 2.11).

Figure 2.11 Split Window View

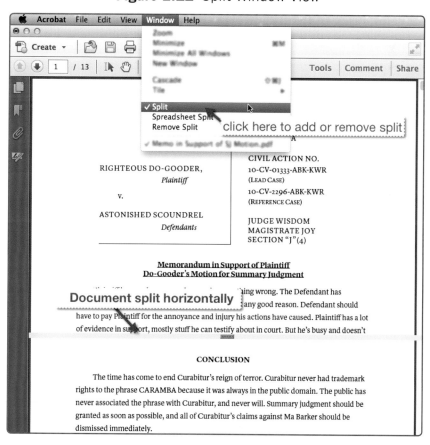

You can remove the split by unchecking Split, using the menu command **Remove Split**, or double-clicking on the split line.

2.8 Read Mode

If you need as much of your screen as possible to read a PDF—perhaps you're using a laptop with small display area—you can hide all the toolbars and task panes using **Read Mode**. To enter Read Mode, choose ***View > Read Mode*** or click the Read Mode button in the upper-right corner of the toolbar.

The button looks like this:

Once you're in Read Mode, you'll see controls, such as page navigation and zoom, appear in a semi-transparent floating toolbar near the bottom of the window (see Figure 2.12).

Figure 2.12 Read Mode Controls

To restore the work area to its previous view, choose ***View > Read Mode*** again. You can also click the **Home** button in far right of the floating toolbar, or hit the **Escape** key.

You may have noticed that Read Mode is the default viewing mode when you open a PDF in a web browser.

Navigating PDFs

Being able to easily and quickly move around a PDF is crucial. We're talking now about page navigation, having already covered zooming and page views. There are several ways to move from page to page, or to jump from one page to a nonadjacent page. We're going to talk about the ways that are most efficient.

3.1 Page Navigation

Most of the time, you'll be moving from one page to the next page or the previous page. The most obvious way is to use the scroll bar on the right-hand side; this is a familiar navigational tool that's present in every program. You can also use the menu to move from page to page, but this is the least efficient way. If you have lots of time, choose **View > Page Navigation** and then one of the choices that follows: **First Page**, **Previous Page**, **Next Page**, or **Last Page**.

Another efficient way to move around is to use the default tools that are in the **Common Tools** area of the toolbar (discussed in Section 4). As seen in Figure 3.1, click the **up arrow** to move to the previous page or the **down arrow** to move to the next page.

Figure 3.1 Default Page Navigation Toobar

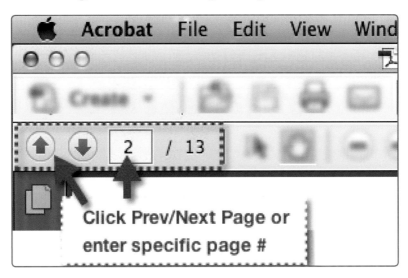

You will probably want to add the additional tools suggested in Section 4, and in that case your toolbar will look like this.

Figure 3.2 Suggested Additions to Toolbar

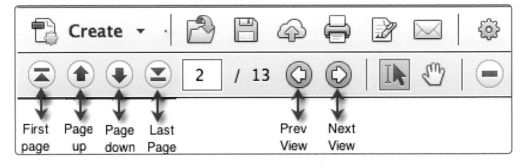

Enabling the tool for **Previous View** is helpful in those instances where you have jumped to a distant page (or perhaps you clicked on a link that took you there), and now you want to jump back. The Previous View tool is like the Back button on a web browser. It immediately returns you to the place you just came from.

You should definitely memorize the keyboard shortcut for jumping back to a previous view: **CMD/CTRL + left arrow** key. In some cases, you may be able to use a Function key combo to do the same thing: **Fn** + **left arrow** key.

Now that you know how to go from page to page, let's learn to jump to specific pages. As Figure 3.2 shows, one way to go to a specific page is to enter the page number in the box (where the number 2 appears) and hit the Enter or Return key. But that requires you to carefully place your cursor into that box, which can quickly become annoying if you're doing a lot of jumping around. Once again, knowing the shortcut is helpful: **CMD/CTRL + Shift + N**, enter the page number, and hit *Enter* or *Return*. Takes about 2.3 seconds (and I know because I timed myself). This is the default technique to adopt, because it'll make a huge difference when you start working a lot with PDFs.

Now you know most of what you need to know about navigating around a PDF. Bookmarks are another way you can navigate, but not all PDFs have bookmarks, so we'll talk about that in Section 8, when we learn how to create and work with bookmarks.

3.2 Screen Navigation

If you are viewing a PDF with the Zoom set to Fit Width, you'll want to navigate through the document one screen at a time. There are several ways to do this. One is to use the scroll wheel on your mouse (see Figure 3.3). Another, often faster, way is to use your mouse to click in the scroll bar, in the area just below the indicator that shows where you are in the document.

Figure 3.3 Scroll Bar Navigation

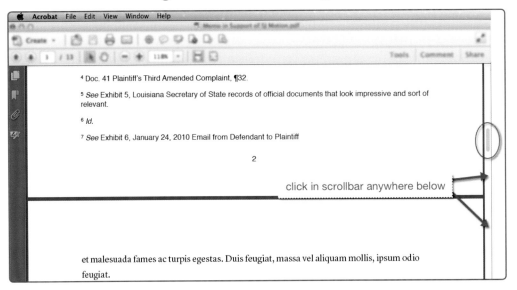

A better way is to use your keyboard. Try the **down arrow**, or **Fn +
down arrow**. The best keyboard shortcut for moving from one screen
of information to another is one that's pretty much universal across all
applications: hit the space bar. And if you want to move up, use **Shift +
Space bar.**

Seriously, this works in most applications (e.g., browsers, word
processors, etc.) on Macs and PCs. Train yourself to use this until it
becomes instinct.

If you are using the shortcut and the pages aren't moving, click in the
Document Pane to make sure that's the focus of your commands. If you're
using one of the other panes, the keyboard shortcut will be focused on
that pane and thus won't navigate the document screen.

The Interface: Menus and Toolbars

Understanding the basic layout of Acrobat is important. You need to know how to access the tools you use most, and how to customize the interface to make those tools easier to get to. **Caveat lector**: the process of customizing the toolbars is tedious, and you won't likely want to do it more than once. Take the time to do it now, while you're reading this book.

4.1 Overview

The overall interface for Adobe Acrobat can be broken down into four main sections: (1) **Menus** and **Toolbars**, (2) **Navigation Pane**, (3) **Document Pane**, and (4) **Task Pane**. Of these four, the Document Pane needs no explanation whatsoever: it's simply the area where the document, or a particular view of it, is displayed. All four areas are shown in Figure 4.1.

Figure 4.1 Main Interface Elements

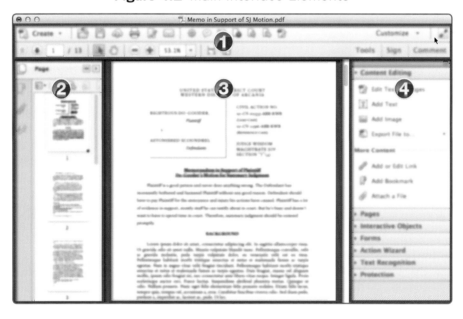

The three areas that surround the Document Pane will be addressed in terms of the tools that they contain.

4.2 Menus and Toolbars

For the novice Acrobat user, the logical place to start is with the menus, which run across the top of the program's window. Acrobat's interface is pretty much the same whether you use a PC or a Mac, as shown in Figure 4.2.

Figure **4.2** PC View and Mac View

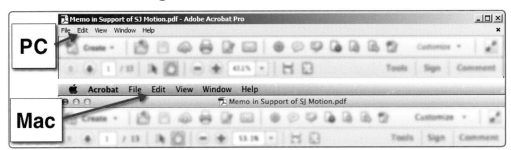

The only noticeable difference is that the Mac has its menu commands slightly farther to the right and in slightly larger font size. Many of the commands you need to use will come from the menu choices you see in Figure 4.2 (e.g., **File**, **Edit**, **View**, **Window**).

Before we take a look at the Task menus, let's see what's available in the **Toobar,** which is the area just below the main menus, as shown in Figure 4.3.

Figure **4.3** Toolbar Area

Each icon represents a commonly used action, often invoked by making one or more menu choices. But instead of having to navigate through several menu selections, you can simply click on the appropriate icon for the command you need at the moment.

The toolbar contains two types of tools: **Common Tools** and **Quick Tools**. The areas containing each type are shown in Figure 4.4.

Figure 4.4 Common Tool Area and Quick Tool Area

The toolbar can be configured by removing, adding, or repositioning the icons, but making these changes is daunting unless you are patient and armed with a clear guidebook. The passages that follow will, hopefully, provide the guidance you need. Before we begin, let me warn you that the manner of reconfiguring the toolbar is not consistent and is often counterintuitive. But you'll only be doing this once, when you first install Acrobat, so let's get started.

4.3 Task Pane

The Task Pane is the area containing three Task menus, which appears on the far right of Acrobat's main interface. We'll talk about the menus and tools in the Task Pane later, but for now take a moment to get familiar with the basic look and feel of this important area.

By the way, the Task menus are slightly different in Acrobat X and Acrobat XI. The screenshot in Figure 4.5 is taken from Acrobat XI. (In the earlier edition, the three menus would be Tools, Comment, Share).

When you click on the Tools menu, a series of choices having to do with **Content Editing** is revealed. Below that drop-down are more options, such as **Pages, Interactive Objects, Forms,** and **Action Wizard**. By default, Acrobat displays only one drop-down menu at a time. When you open a drop-down, Acrobat closes the menu that was previously open. So, if you now clicked on Pages, the Task Pane would close Content Editing and open up a Pages menu, as shown in Figure 4.6.

Figure 4.5 Task Menus

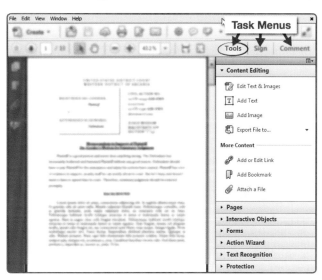

Figure 4.6 Pages Menu

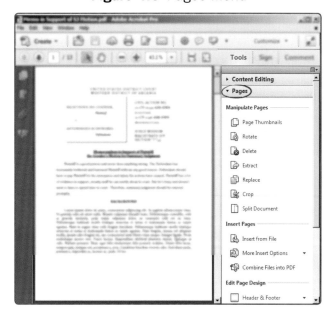

4.4 The Options Menu

You can add more tool sets to the Tools menu by using the little **Options** menu, as shown in Figure 4.7.

Figure 4.7 Options Menu

Any tool set that has a check mark will be displayed; those that are not checked are hidden. You should go see what's hidden in your Options menu. Maybe you'll find something useful.

4.5 Editing the Common Tools

Editing the **Common Tools** is simple. Hover your cursor over the area where the Common Tools are located. Some of the icons will display a yellow pop-up box when you keep the cursor over them for a couple of seconds. Hover over the hand icon to see what happens; it should be something like the picture in Figure 4.8.

Figure 4.8 Editing Common Tools

Once you've learned to hover to see what the various icons are, you're ready to start modifying the toolbar to add icons for new tools in the Common Tools area. For this you need to use the right-click technique. Let's say you have your cursor over the hand icon (but it doesn't really matter which icon, as long as it's in the Common Tools area). When you right-click, you will see the menu shown in Figure 4.9.

Figure 4.9 Right-Click to Reveal Options

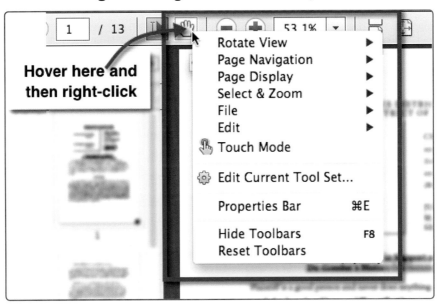

The next step is to pick one of the general options, such as Rotate View or Page Navigation. At that point, you'll be able to add the tools you want by selecting it, and the new icon will appear on the toolbar. You can remove the tool by right-clicking in the toolbar and selecting that tool again. Most people seem to appreciate having the tools shown in Figure 4.10 on the toolbar, so you might want to add these to the Common Tools toolbar.

You don't get to choose where the added tools are positioned; Acrobat puts them in exactly the spot shown and you can't alter it. In fact, that's pretty much how it works for

Figure 4.10 Recommended Tools

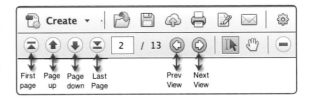

all of the Common Tools. You have more control over the next set of tools, but unfortunately the way of adding them is completely different from the method you just learned.

4.6 Editing the Quick Tools

Quick Tools are more specialized tools that the folks at Adobe figure most users will want to have close at hand. But "most users" doesn't mean "most lawyers," so you're going to want to change this toolbar to your liking.

To make changes to the toolbar, you either (1) click the gear icon next to the red arrow, as shown in Figure 4.11, or (2) right-click anywhere in the toolbar. Doing so will call up a contextual menu from which you can make changes by selecting ***Quick Tools*** (Acrobat X) or ***Edit Current Tool Set*** (Acrobat XI), which is the option shown in Figure 4.11.

Figure 4.11 Option to Edit Quick Tools

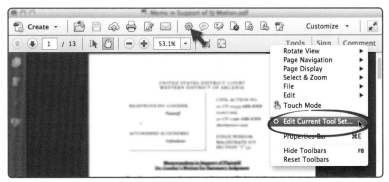

Next, you'll be able to make a series of selections to add all the icons you want at once. You can also arrange the icons in the order you prefer. All of this is done from the dialog box that appears after you've selected the ***Edit Current Tool Set*** option.

Figure 4.12 Editing Quick Tools

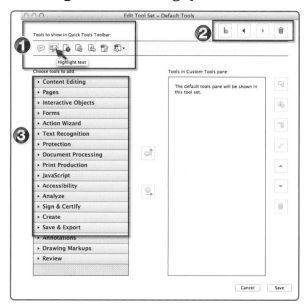

In area 1, you see the tools that have been preloaded into the Quick Tools toolbar. To determine what each icon does, simply hover your cursor over the one you're curious about and you'll see a yellow pop-up box. The one in Figure 4.12 appeared when I hovered over the icon for highlighting text.

If you want to move these icons around or delete them, use the tools in area 2. You can load new Quick Tools by making choices in area 3 and then using the options in area 2 to arrange the icons in the order you prefer. Granted, it can seem a bit tedious to corral all the options you want, and when you're starting out it's often hard to know which Quick Tools you are going to want most.

The following options are the ones legal professionals tend to use most frequently.

Pages Tools Menu

- **Extract.** Allows you to extract a page, or range of pages
- **Split Document.** Allows you to split a PDF by top-level book-marks (great when you have one big PDF that actually contains many separate documents; we'll discuss this in Section 8)
- **Bates Numbering.** Gives you a dialog box to select choices related to Bates stamping documents (Pro version only)

Content Tools Menu

- **Edit Document Text.** Allows for mostly minor changes to text in a PDF that's text searchable
- **Add or Edit Text Box.** Allows you superimpose text onto a PDF or edit text that's already been added. This tool used to be known as the **Typewriter** tool, because it lets you fill in PDF forms that are simply scans of form documents. In other words, you're using the Acrobat version of a typewriter to add text. An exceptionally useful tool.

Recognize Text Menu

- **In This File.** Allows OCR (optical character recognition; discussed in Section 11), or makes the current PDF into a text-searchable PDF

Protection Tools Menu

- **Mark for Redaction.** Enables selection of designated page areas, or text, to be redacted according to specified choices
- **Apply Redactions.** Makes all areas marked for redaction permanently obscured, with designated text notations if desired

Annotations Menu

- **Stamps Tool.** Lets you quickly stamp your digital signature (discussed in Section 12)

4.7 Navigation Pane

The **Navigation Pane** is important because, as the name implies, it provides a couple of useful tools for getting around a PDF quickly. There are four side tabs in this pane: (1) **Page Thumbnails**, (2) **Bookmarks**, (3) **Attachments**, and (4) **Signatures**.

The last two have nothing really to do with navigation, but that's where Adobe put them.

Figure 4.13 Navigation Pane Choices

The **Page Thumbnails** option is helpful for navigating PDFs based on thumbnail views of each page, but mostly it is used to rearrange pages quickly. The Page Thumbnails view is displayed in Figure 4.14, which shows the Navigation Pane surrounded by a red rectangle.

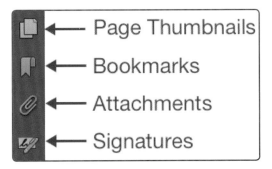

Figure 4.14 Page Thumbnails View

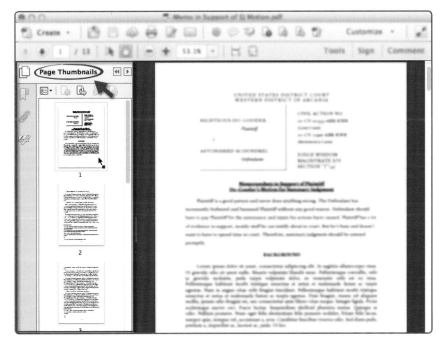

Page Thumbnails will be covered in more detail in Section 7.1, but for now, just know that this is the best place to rearrange pages in a PDF.

Probably most useful tool in the Navigation Pane is Bookmarks, and it's one of the first tools you should learn to use well. Bookmarks will be covered in detail later (Section 8). Basically, they're like the sticky tabs that people put in stacks of paper to mark important pages. In their most rudimentary application, bookmarks in PDFs are basically hyperlinks to particular pages or to a zoomed view on a specific page. Bookmarks can also be used as a table of contents; for example, for the headings in a memorandum in support of a motion, as shown in Figure 4.15.

Figure 4.15 Bookmarks View

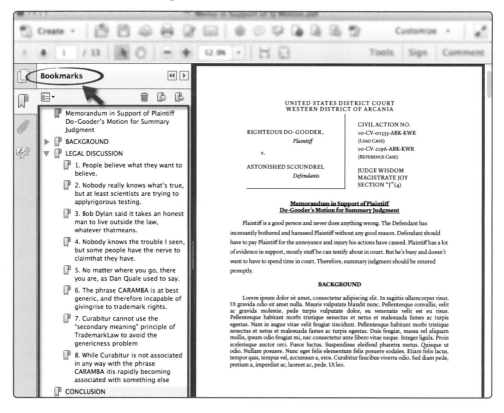

Creating PDFs

PDFs can be created in many ways, but the goal in each case is the same: to produce a PDF with the highest resolution, smallest file size, and greatest functionality. Fortunately, the most common ways of creating PDFs will accomplish all of those things without any special effort on your part. The process for creating PDFs starts with one of two options: (1) the **Create** button on the toolbar or (2) the menu selection *File > Create*. And as you can see in Figure 5.1, either method provides the same choices.

Figure 5.1 Options for Creating a PDF

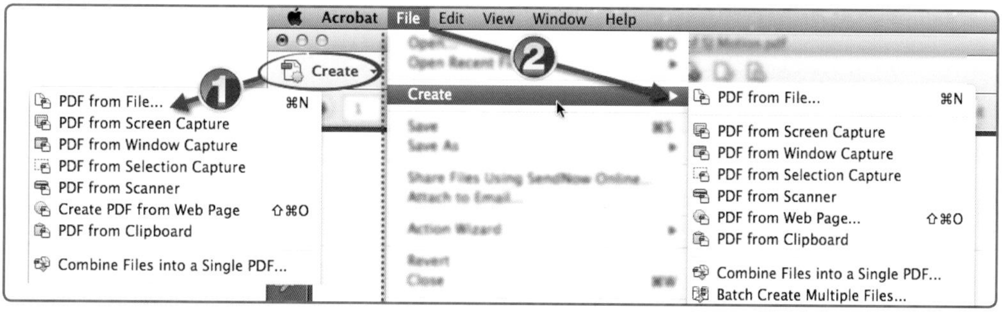

We'll talk about each of these options, but first let's discuss how to create a PDF from another application, such as Microsoft Word.

5.1 PDF Creator on PC

When using a Microsoft Office application on a PC, such as Word, always use the PDF Creator tool to create a PDF. That option is located under the **Adobe** menu in Word's ribbon. Using this option will ensure the resulting PDF carries over the maximum amount of formatting information. So, if you use **Styles** in your Word documents (and you should!), those style markers will become hierarchical bookmarks. We'll cover why bookmarks are supremely useful in Section 8.

A screenshot of the PDF Creator tool in the Adobe ribbon is shown in Figure 5.2.

Figure 5.2 Adobe PDF Creator in Microsoft Word

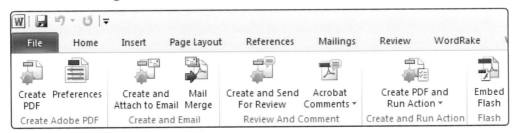

To create a PDF from the Adobe ribbon simply click the **Create PDF** icon. Using the PDF Creator is the fastest, and easiest, method of creating a PDF. Again, it's *always* the preferred method.

5.2 "Print to PDF" on PC

In some cases, you may have to select a printer named "Adobe PDF" to create a file. This used to be the dominant method on Windows computers, which is why you often hear the term "print to PDF." If you're trying to create a PDF from an application other than Microsoft Office, you might have to resort to this method, but in general you should avoid it. The problem is that it takes longer and will strip out useful features such as hyperlinks.

However, in some cases you will want to use this method to "flatten" a signature stamp, as described in Section 12.5. Otherwise, avoid this method if you can.

5.3 "Save as PDF" on Mac

On a Mac, here's the PDF conversion process: (1) choose *File > Print* to reveal a dialog box where you can (2) select *Save as PDF* (see Figure 5.3).

Figure 5.3 Creating PDFs on a Mac

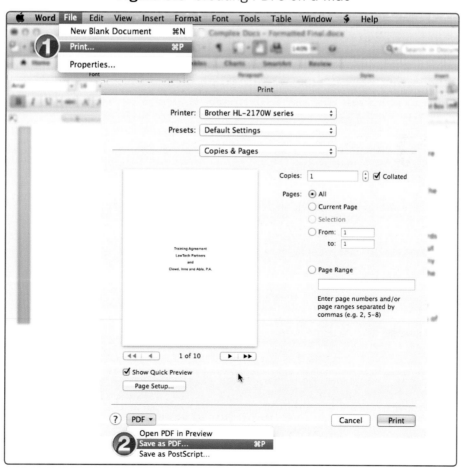

Having to make two separate selections can be frustrating if you're creating a lot of PDFs on the Mac. If you want to create a keyboard shortcut that will speed the process up, a lawyer named David Sparks has written an excellent online tutorial, which is available at http://is.gd/Tu8xhl.

Creating PDFs in the fashion just described will cause the resulting PDF to lose hyperlinks and styles if you're using Microsoft Word. You can preserve those features using the method explained in Section 8.11.

5.4 Printing the Current Page

You probably don't need instructions on how to print to a regular printer (the kind with *real* paper). So, we're not going to cover that. Instead, I'll mention something I often have to remind myself of: the option to print only the current page. A lot of times you'll open a PDF and find that you have to print out one particular page. But in your haste you wind up printing the whole PDF.

From now on, print only the page that you truly need by selecting the **Current page** option (see Figure 5.4).

Figure 5.4 Consider Printing Just One Page

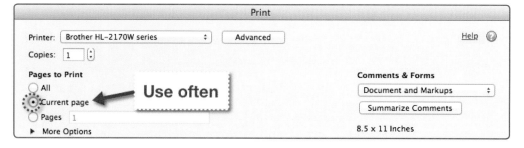

Maybe even take a screenshot of this dialog box and print *that* out to remind you. Think of the trees.

5.5 Converting Files to PDF

Often you will encounter a file that you need to convert to a PDF, but you don't have the native program that opens the file (or you don't want to bother opening it just to create a PDF). In that situation, either (1) select *File > Create* and choose *PDF from File* or (2) use the toolbar option (see Figure 5.5).

Figure 5.5 Converting Non-PDF File into PDF

Then select the file that you want to convert and click **Open**. Depending on the type of file being converted, the authoring application will open automatically or a dialog box showing progress may appear. If the file is in an unsupported format, a message appears telling you that the file cannot be converted. However, you will be able to convert most common file types with this option.

5.6 Scanning to PDF

You can create a PDF file by using a scanner and Acrobat. The process for doing this is: *Select File > Create PDF > From Scanner*. And remember, PDFs that are created using a scanner will not initially be text-searchable. To make them searchable you'll have to use the **Recognize Text** option in the **Task Pane**, which we'll talk about in Section 11.

In general, the software that comes with your scanner will determine how you scan and what settings you can use, and sometimes it will offer an option to apply OCR to the text (i.e., make it searchable during the scan process). There are many different types of scanners available these days, and no doubt many of them will meet your needs. However, as a busy lawyer, make sure you have something robust and reliable.

For what it's worth, I have used a version of **Fujitsu's ScanSnap** scanner and found it consistently reliable. I appreciate its fifty-page document feeder and its ability to scan mixed-size paper and capture both the front and back in one pass. As of this writing, the most current model is the iX500, which comes with a full version of Acrobat Standard for Windows. Being able to easily and quickly scan paper documents is essential in a law practice; so don't try to cut corners when it comes to purchasing a scanner.

5.7 Combining Files to PDF

A common scenario in the modern law firm is this: you want to merge a group of PDFs into a single PDF document. Or perhaps you want to merge a bunch of different file types into a single PDF document. No problem. Acrobat can help you out.

Use the following process: select *File > Create > Combine Files into a Single PDF*.

If a PDF document is already open in Acrobat, it will appear in the list of included files. In the upper right corner of the *Combine Files* dialog box, double-check that *Single PDF* is selected. Then, from the *Add Files* menu, you will be given the option to add individual files (select the desired files) or to add all the files in a folder (choose *Add Folders*, then select the desired folder). Once you've got the files loaded in the dialog box in the order you want, just click *Combine Files*. Then you'll be prompted to name the document and save it.

If you've used the federal court e-filing system (or perhaps a similar state e-filing system), you've discovered that a single motion filed by your opponent generates multiple PDFs (e.g., Motion, Memo in Support, Notice of Submission, Proposed Order, and Exhibits). You probably don't want to manage all those documents as separate PDFs. So, use this merging process to combine all the files into a single PDF.

Remember, the order of the PDFs can be controlled in the dialog box. You can move any document up to the top so it's the first document in the resulting PDF. In Figure 5.6 below, the main document is labeled as such and needs to be first in the PDF. It can be moved up by selecting the file and then using the green **up arrow** tool (circled).

Figure 5.6 Combining PDFs

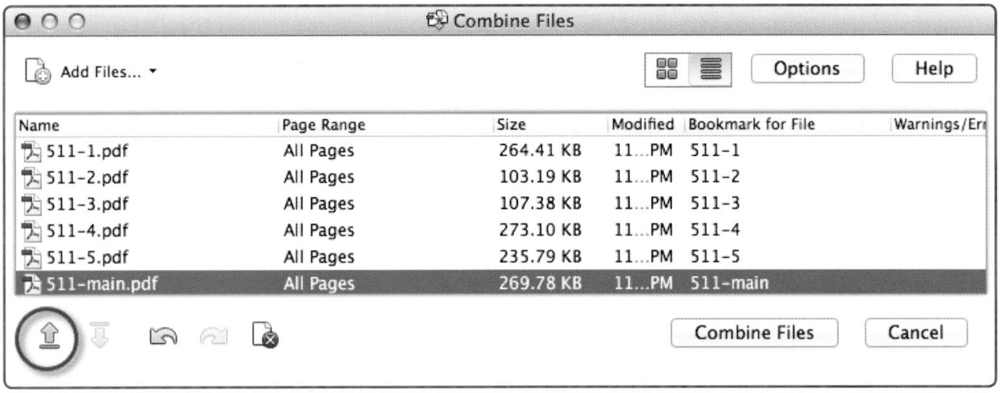

If you had PDFs already open that you wanted to combine, you would go to the ***Add Files*** menu (top left in the dialog box), choose ***Add Open Files***, and then select the open PDFs.

What happens if you have loaded a lot of documents and need to move them around? This often occurs when you're combining a bunch of exhibits together, perhaps to e-file as one PDF. In Figure 5.7, you'll notice that the files were loaded based on an alphanumeric sort order.

Figure 5.7 Deselecting to Allow Rearranging of PDFs

For the exhibits to load in sequential sort order, you'd have to have named the files Exhibit 01, Exhibit 02, and so on for exhibits 1 through 9. But for now, you want to move them around. Often when all of the files are selected (everything in blue), you can't then select just one to move it. To fix that, you'll have to expand the dialog box by positioning your cursor along the bottom until you see dual arrows (one facing up and one down). Then you can drag the bottom border down to create more space, as shown in Figure 5.7. Click in the white space to deselect the files you just added.

Once you've deselected all the files, you'll be able to select any one of them individually and move it around as you desire. As you can see, this can be a laborious process. I recommend you make it a practice to add the leading zeros to filenames for exhibits so you don't have to move things around in the dialog box.

5.8 Screen Capture to PDF (Mac only)

If you're using Acrobat on a Mac, you can also do a screen capture of a computer window or a select area in the display and create a PDF from that capture. To do this, select ***File > Create*** and then one of these options: **PDF from Screen Capture**, **PDF from Window Capture**, or **PDF from Selection Capture.**

Sometimes this can be handy for capturing something on a web page. Just make sure to capture enough information to help you authenticate the document. If you need more than just one page or area of a website, you'll have to use a more robust capture tool, one designed specifically for websites. In that case, read on.

5.9 Web Capture to PDF

Acrobat has the ability to capture sections of a website, or even an entire website. You can convert an open web page to a PDF from Internet Explorer or Firefox (also Chrome and Safari in Acrobat XI), but you get more options when converting from within Acrobat. For example, you can include an entire website in the resulting PDF or just some levels of the site.

Select ***File > Create > PDF from Web Page***. At this point, you'll have to enter the web page's URL. To change the number of levels in the website to convert, expand ***Capture Multiple Levels***. Enter the number of levels to include or select ***Get Entire Site*** to include all levels from the website.

5.10 Create Multiple PDFs from Mulitple Files

You can create multiple PDFs from multiple native files (assuming they are of a type that Acrobat can convert) in a one-batch operation. This comes in handy when you have to convert many non-PDF files. Begin by choosing *File > Create > Batch Create Multiple Files*.

Then, select *Add Files > Add Files or Add Folders* and the files or folders you want to convert. Click *OK*. An options dialog box will appear, and you can then select the target folder and filename preferences.

5.11 Creating PDFs from an E-mail Program

If you're using a PC and you use Microsoft Outlook or Lotus Notes as your e-mail program, you can convert e-mails directly to PDF. This is a Windows-only feature.

You'll know that you have this option if, in Outlook or Lotus Notes, you see the **Adobe PDF** tab, as shown in Figure 5.8, which is where you begin the process of converting selected e-mails to PDF in Outlook (the process is the same in Lotus Notes).

Figure 5.8 Converting Microsoft Outlook E-mails to PDF

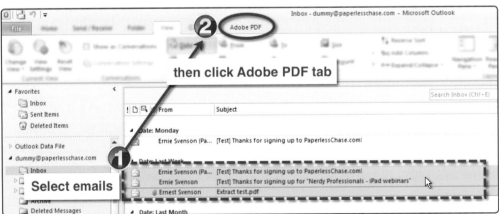

Once you've selected the e-mails and clicked the **Adobe PDF** tab, you'll see the screen shown in Figure 5.9 in Outlook.

Figure 5.9 Selecting E-mails to Be Converted

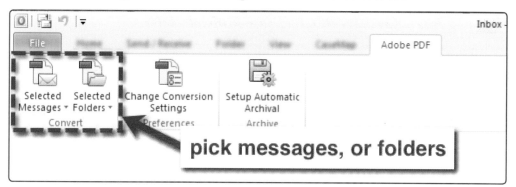

You have the option to convert selected messages (each of which you must manually select) or to convert entire e-mail folders. Once the conversion has taken place, you simply choose where to save the resulting PDF. The file will contain the e-mails and also embed any attachments, which can be opened if you have the program associated with them (just as would be the case if you were trying to open an attachment from within Outlook or Lotus Notes).

Converting e-mails to PDF from within Outlook or Lotus Notes is a powerful feature and one that you should try just so you can get a sense of how it works. Many lawyers who use Outlook or Lotus Notes on a PC find it incredibly useful.

Section 6

Examining PDFs

We're going to talk about how to manipulate PDFs in the most common and useful ways. Before we do, let's quickly look at how you can tell what kind of PDF you have open. Sometimes you'll get a PDF that's locked down in ways that prevent you from manipulating it. Weirdly, this seems to be the case with many PDFs that come from court reporters and government agencies, usually when it makes no sense to lock down the files.

6.1 Document Description

To quickly examine PDFs you need to work with, you can open *File > Properties*, or you can use the keyboard shortcut: **CMD/CTRL + D**. Then, you'll see a dialog box like the one in Figure 6.1.

Let's begin by clicking on the **Description** tab, as shown in Figure 6.1. Once you've done that, you'll see some basic metadata, such as (1) the file-name, title, and author; (2) the document creation date, when it was last modified, and what program was used to create it (in this example, Apple's word processing program, Pages); (3) an option for examining more metadata (usually not that useful); and (4) the file size, page size, and how many pages the PDF contains.

Figure 6.1 Examining PDF Properties

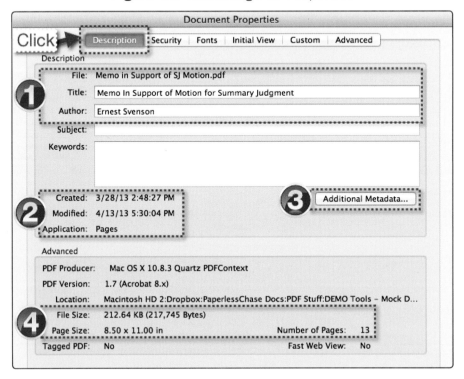

6.2 Document Security

Now go back up and click the **Security** tab, which will reveal the information shown in Figure 6.2 and let you know if the PDF was locked down in any way.

Figure 6.2 Examining PDF Security Settings

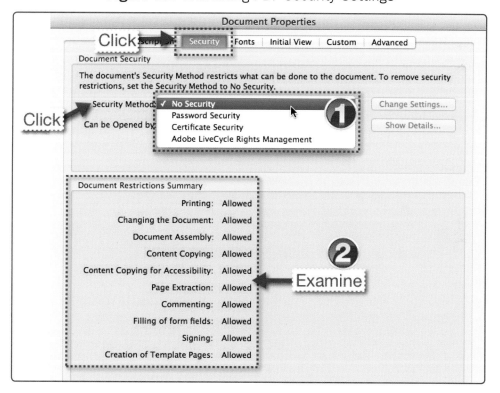

After you click the **Security** tab, you can (1) examine the **Security Method** drop-down menu (this document has "No Security") and (2) see the **Document Restrictions** (you'll see all the options that are still enabled). We'll cover how to apply security to a document in Section 18.

For now, you should know that by applying document restrictions you can prevent someone from doing the following:

- printing (disable completely the ability to print the PDF; limit printing to either high resolution or low resolution)
- changing the document (prevent any change whatsoever; selectively disable inserting, deleting, or rotating pages; commenting; filling form fields; digital signing)
- copying content (prevent use of the selection tool to copy text or images)

By examining the Document Restrictions, you can quickly see what operations have been allowed or disallowed. If you receive a PDF and are having trouble doing any operations, check the Document Properties dialog box immediately.

Section 7

Pages

Back in Section 3, we briefly talked about page navigation in PDF documents. Now we're going to talk about manipulating PDFs, starting with page manipulation. We're going to do things to PDF pages that go beyond mere navigation. And we're going to start by returning to the Navigation Pane that we touched on in Section 4. Click on the **Page Thumbnails** icon to reveal the **Navigation Pane** for pages (see Figure 7.1).

Figure 7.1 Rearranging Pages

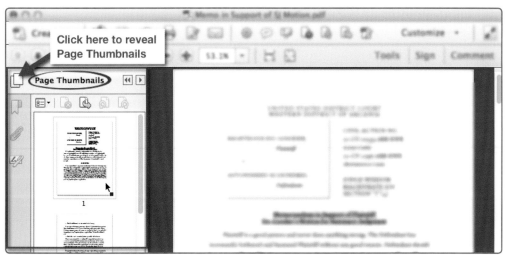

From here, you could navigate from one page to another by clicking on the thumbnail for the page you wanted to jump to. This is another way to navigate through pages, but there are so many more things you can do with PDF pages, and that's the real focus of this section.

7.1 Rearranging

Often you'll want to move a page to a new location. The best way to do that is here in the **Page Thumbnails** view of the Navigation Pane. But what if the thumbnails you see in this view are too small? Simply click on the *Options* menu (a small page icon) in the Navigation Pane, as shown in Figure 7.2, and then select *Enlarge Page Thumbnails*. (If you wanted to make the thumbnails smaller, you'd select the option above it.)

Figure 7.2 Enlarging Page Thumbnails

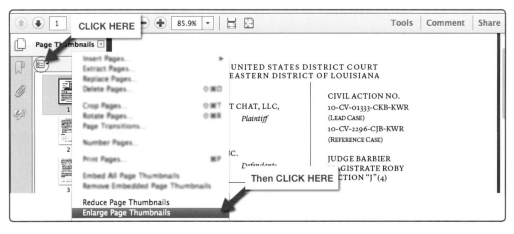

What if you have lots of pages you need to move around, and you need to see lots of thumbnails? Simply put your cursor in the area between the Page Thumbnails view and the Document Pane and drag to the right, as shown in Figure 7.3.

Figure 7.3 Increasing Size of Page Thumbnail View Area

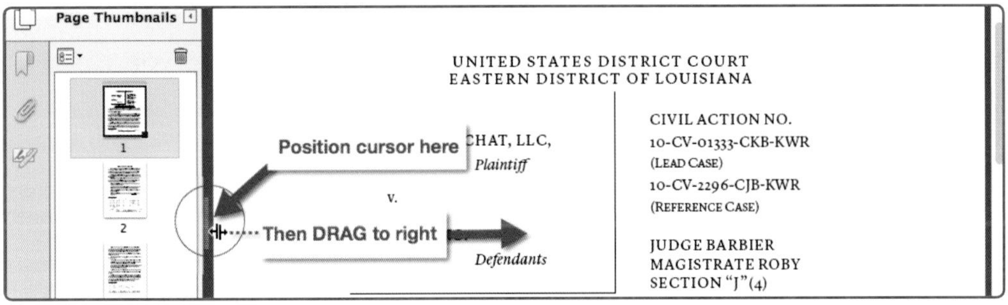

Then you'll see a view somewhat like the one in Figure 7.4, which makes it easy to move a page to the correct location.

Figure 7.4 Drag to Move a Page

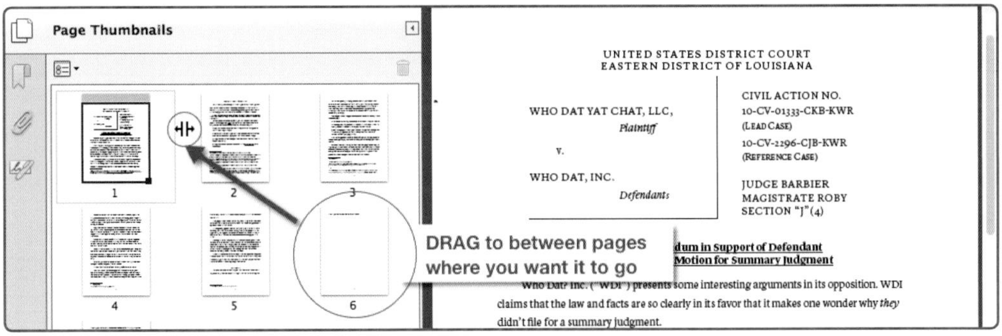

To move a page, select it with your cursor and then drag and drop it in the newly desired location. To move more than one page, select the first page in the range and press and hold down the Shift key and then select the last page in the range. From there, you can drag and drop as just described.

While it's easy to rearrange a few pages in a PDF, you'll find that moving lots of pages around is difficult and extremely annoying. So the best practice is to arrange pages the way you need them to be *before* you create the PDF (by scanning or printing to PDF). The method explained here is one you'll use when you didn't control how the PDF pages were arranged.

7.2 Inserting

You can insert pages in a number of ways. If you like using toolbars, you can put the **Insert Pages** tool into the toolbar using the method that we covered in Section 4. Or you can use the drop-down menu in the Page Thumbnails view that we just talked about, but this time you'd select *Insert Pages*.

Figure 7.5 Inserting Pages into a PDF—Option #1

As you can see, you have three basic options. First, you can insert a page from a file; usually that will be another PDF, but it could be any type of file that Acrobat will import (you'll see your choices when you make the selection). Second, you can import whatever is in the clipboard; for example, you can take a screenshot of something and then quickly insert it into a PDF as a new page. Third, you can insert a blank page, which is useful when you want to create separator pages. And, as we'll discuss in Section 10, you also have the ability to insert text into a PDF, so doing that to a blank page would be a quick (but not elegant) way to create tabs for a trial notebook, or for a document set.

Another way to insert pages into a PDF is to use the Task Pane, shown on the right side in Figure 7.6. Simply select **Tools > Pages** and then **Insert from File**. The choice will default to only PDF files, but in the dialog box you can choose to show all files and then pull in (and have converted to PDF) one of the other supported file types.

Also, you can choose additional options by clicking on **More Insert Options**, also shown in Figure 7.6.

Figure 7.6 Inserting Pages into a PDF—Option #2

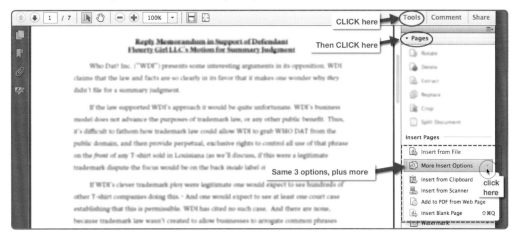

Notice that in addition to the three options we talked about already, you have some more, including **Insert from Scanner** and **Add to PDF from Web Page**. You'll be able to use the scanner insert option only if you have a TWAIN compatible scanner (if you're interested in knowing what TWAIN stands for, or what it is, just check the Wikipedia discussion). As a practical matter, most people don't need to scan pages into an existing PDF or add to a PDF from web pages, so those choices aren't often used—which is probably why Adobe hid them so well.

About 99 percent of the time, lawyers will want to select Insert Pages to add PDF pages into an existing PDF document.

7.3 Create a PDF from a Blank Page

You can create a PDF from a blank page rather than beginning with a file, a clipboard image, or scanning.

This process creates a one-page PDF. To start, close any open documents (otherwise the program will insert a blank page in the current document). On a PC, open the *Task Pane* and select *Tools > Pages > More Insert Options > Insert Blank Page*.

Repeated use of the Insert Blank Page command will add more blank pages to the existing PDF.

On a Mac, you won't be able to access the **Task Pane** if you don't have a document open. There is a keyboard shortcut for inserting a blank page (and it changed from Acrobat X to Acrobat XI). In Acrobat XI, it is **CMD + Shift + T**. In Acrobat X, it's **CMD + Shift + Q**.

7.4 Extracting

When you want to copy a few select pages from a PDF, use the **Extract** command. You can invoke this command from the same three places we mentioned for inserting pages: (1) the toolbar, (2) the Page Thumbnails view, and (3) the Task Pane. Extracting pages is something most lawyers and legal professionals do frequently, and it's pretty easy to figure out how to do it without any instruction at all.

When you use the Extract command, you'll get a dialog box that lets you pick the page range you want to extract and offers two other options, as shown in the screenshot in Figure 7.7.

The main thing to remember is, unless you select the **Delete Pages After Extracting** option, you're only extracting *copies* of the pages you want (usually, that's what you want). You can also extract pages so that each one is a separate file, which is probably not something most people

Figure 7.7 Extracting Pages

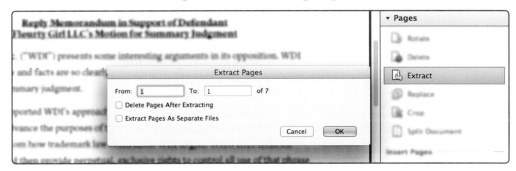

will ever do. But it's an option, so keep in mind that you have the ability to do it, in case you ever need to.

7.5 Deleting

Deleting pages is easy. If you want to delete a bunch of pages and you need to see what the pages look like, use the Page Thumbnails view. If you know the page range and don't need to look at the pages to decide which ones need deleting (which is usually my situation), use the Task Pane and select *Tools > Pages > Delete*.

Frankly, deleting pages is something you'll be doing often, so I recommend you memorize the keyboard shortcut, which is **CMD/CTRL + Shift + D**. This shortcut is so fundamental that it's included in the "Keyboard Shortcut Cheat Sheet" in the Appendix.

7.6 Replacing

You can find the **Replace** command in the three places we've been talking about (although you'll have to add it to the toolbar using the process we described in Section 4 if you want to do it from there).

Replacing pages isn't something that comes up as much as inserting or extracting them, but it's useful every now and then. One way it might come up is if you need to make changes to a PDF page that you created from a word processing program. Perhaps you have manipulated the PDF by adding bookmarks or other comments, and simply re-creating the PDF isn't the best option.

You can edit the word processing document and "print to PDF" just the one page you need to replace. Then use the Replace command to swap out the new page for the old one (you can replace only one page at a time, not a range of pages). Obviously, you could delete the old page and then insert the new page, but the Replace command is designed for this situation, so why not use it?

7.7 Rotating

Being able to rotate pages is a key skill and one you'll want to master fully. Many people, for whatever reason, send out PDFs with random pages incorrectly rotated. Perhaps they scanned them in improperly, who knows? The thing is, you'll get these types of files, and you'll need to be able to fix them quickly. In Section 2, we covered how to rotate selected pages in a PDF and then lock in the changes.

Here I'll just remind you that the keyboard shortcut is one you'll want to memorize: **CMD/CTRL + Shift + R**. This is another fundamental shortcut; hence, I include it my "Keyboard Shortcut Cheat Sheet" in the Appendix.

7.8 Cropping

Cropping pages is something you might need to do from time to time, typically when you have a document that has marginalia at the edges that you need to remove (e.g., a fax number or weird web address info in the document footer of a web page that was printed out). You can access the **Crop** command from all three of the places we've talked about.

The process for cropping is a multistep one and follows this sequence:

1. Click the ***Crop*** command (your cursor will turn into a crosshair, indicating you can select an area).

2. Select the area you want to leave in the document (in other words, you select the part you want to keep).

3. Double-click inside the area you selected and you'll get a dialog box that looks like Figure 7.8.

Figure 7.8 Cropping a PDF

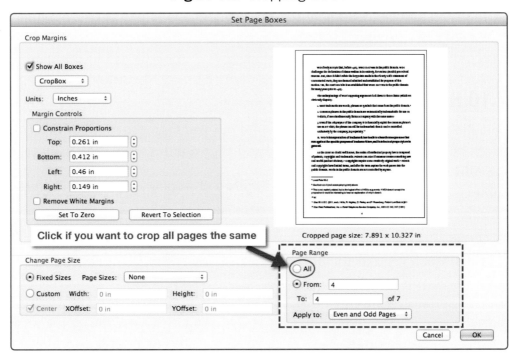

There are lots of options, but the only one that you'll probably care about is the one that lets you specify if you want to crop just the one page or if you want to crop all of the pages in that PDF simultaneously.

Cropping doesn't remove the text that has been cropped out, so if it's sensitive information, it should be redacted using the method that will be described in Section 15.

7.9 Splitting

The page-splitting feature was first introduced in version 9 of Acrobat. This feature allows you to split a multipage PDF into smaller files by using several criteria: (1) number of pages, (2) file size, and (3) top-level bookmarks. For lawyers, the most useful option is 3, the ability to split by top-level bookmarks. I'll address splitting in Section 8, after explaining how bookmarks work.

7.10 Headers and Footers

Sometimes you create a PDF only to find out you forgot to number the pages. No worries; you can physically add page numbers to a PDF using the **Add Headers & Footers** command. Click *Tools > Pages > Header & Footer > Add Header & Footer* (see Figure 7.9).

Then, you'll get a dialog box from which you can choose various options regarding where the numbers appear, what page to start numbering, and what number to use as the first number (see Figure 7.10).

Figure 7.9 Adding Headers or Footers

Figure 7.10 Options for Headers and Footers

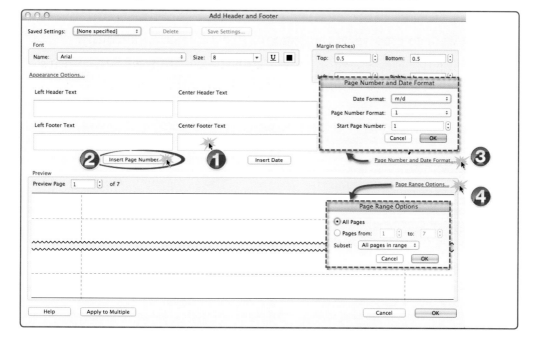

Pick the area of the document you want to put the number in. Usually it will be the bottom middle area. Here's the sequence you want to follow:

1. Click in the panel designated *Center Footer Text*.
2. Then click the button that says *Insert Page Number*.
3. If needed, click the *Page Number and Date Format* link, and choose the options (as shown).
4. If needed, click the *Page Range Options* link, and make desired choices (as shown).

Part II

Intermediate Skills

In the Intermediate Skills section, we're going to build on the key skills you learned in the basics section. Now you'll find out how to manipulate PDFs in basic ways—such as creating comments and bookmarks—that are useful in everyday practice. These skills will help you become super-efficient with PDFs.

Bookmarks

Bookmarks are primarily used as navigational tools. You click on a bookmark and you're immediately taken to the location in the PDF that the bookmark points to. Bookmarks transport you not only to a page but also to a particular *view* on that page. So, if you set the bookmark when the page was zoomed in on a selected page area, then clicking on the bookmark will take you to the page and to that view.

Creating and using bookmarks is the skill that will move you from the realm of novice to power user in dealing with PDFs. Bookmarks are easy to create and use. But, for some reason, many lawyers don't figure out how to incorporate them into their PDF skill set. That's a shame, because bookmarks are one of the most powerful tools at a busy, PDF-using lawyer's disposal. And you're about to find out why.

8.1 Creating Bookmarks

Many bookmarks will be created in the PDF authoring process by using the PDF Creator that is automatically installed in Microsoft Office applications (Windows only). But if you need to create bookmarks in a PDF, there are two primary ways: open the ***Bookmark*** panel from the Navigation Pane (covered in Section 4), use the keyboard shortcut. Since creating bookmarks is such an important skill, I recommend you use only the keyboard shortcut.

But you should see the differences for yourself. Here's the sequence:

1. Click on **Bookmark** icon on **Navigation Pane** (the Bookmark Pane then opens up).

2. Click on the **New Bookmark** icon (see Figure 8.1).

3. Or, pick the **Options Menu** (small page icon) as shown in Figure 8.2.

But, like I said, the best way to create bookmarks is to use the keyboard shortcut. Since I used a Mac computer to create the screenshot for Figure 8.2 you see the shortcut key combo for a Mac. Hopefully, you've cultivated the habit of noticing those keyboard shortcuts in drop-down menus.

Figure 8.1 Bookmarks— Click to Create Icon

Figure 8.2 Bookmarks— Drop Down Menu

Anyway, here is the shortcut you want to commit to memory: **CMD/CTRL + B**. Stare at it and keep repeating it, like a Buddhist monk reciting a mantra.

8.2 Creating Bookmarks the Fast and Easy Way

Whenever I download a brief that's been filed in federal court, the first thing I do is open up the Memorandum in Support and create bookmarks that correspond to each major section and to all the subsections. If the only way to create bookmarks was to type them in by hand, I wouldn't do it. Fortunately, there is an easier way—and it's superfast too.

You need the PDFs you're going to bookmark to be text searchable, which will usually be the case. A text-searchable PDF is one that you can select text from.

Figure 8.3 shows an example of the kind of pleading I'm talking about. It already has two bookmarks, and now we need to create a new one for the subheading numbered 1 ("The Plaintiff doesn't have time to deal with this stuff."). Simply click the **Selection** tool in the toolbar, drag across the text you want to have as the bookmark name, and then invoke the keyboard shortcut for creating a bookmark.

Figure 8.3 Fastest Way to Bookmark a Memo with Headings

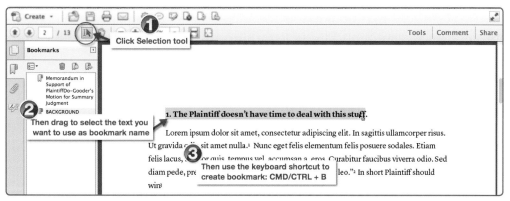

The newly created bookmark will be named exactly the same as the selected text. Using this method, you can easily bookmark an entire brief in a couple of minutes. Then you'll have a nice table of contents of the major parts of the brief your opponent filed.

Figure 8.4 Example with Nested Bookmarks

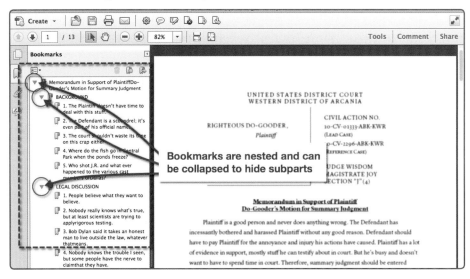

If you noticed that bookmarks for subsections of the brief were nested below main sections (see Figure 8.4), you're probably wondering how that was done.

8.3 Nesting Bookmarks

Nesting bookmarks is easy to do: just position your cursor over the bookmark you want to move and wait until it turns into a little hand with a pointing finger (see Figure 8.5). Then you're ready to drag the bookmark into the nested position.

Figure 8.5 How to Nest a Bookmark

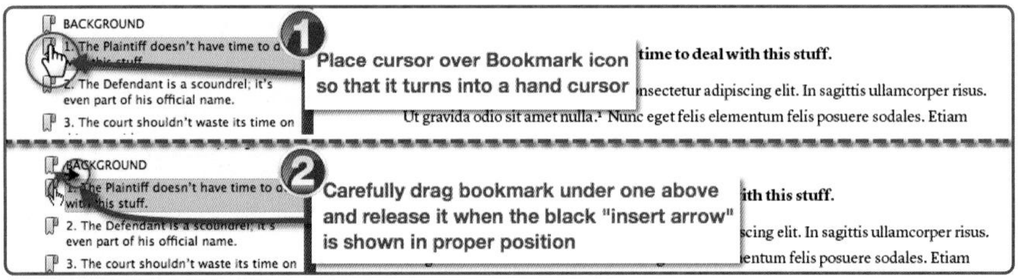

The trick (and believe me, there is an art to this) is to release the bookmark at just the right time. If you release it in the wrong place, it won't nest; it'll stay at the same level it's currently on.

Fortunately, you can nest multiple bookmarks at one time. Select all the bookmarks you want to nest. Then drag them as one unit using the method just described. This makes it easy to quickly nest a group of bookmarks, reducing the agony associated with placing the cursor in the exactly the right place over and over for proper nesting.

To un-nest a bookmark, just reverse the process: drag the bookmark out away from its nested position to the outer level you want to move it to.

If you need to collapse the Bookmarks view, you can do that from the Options menu of the Navigation Pane, as shown in Figure 8.6.

Usually, you'll collapse and expand bookmarks by clicking on the little black arrow next to the bookmark. But you'll encounter some PDFs where the Bookmarks view looks like a thriving shrub forest. In that situation, you'll find the menu option just described to be incredibly useful.

Figure 8.6 Collapse Nested Bookmarks

8.4 Updating a Bookmark's Destination

If you need to make an existing bookmark point to a new location or a new view, you can change its destination. Simply navigate to the page or view that you want the bookmark to point to and then right-click on the bookmark that's to be updated. When you right-click, you'll be presented with a set of contextual options; choose ***Set Destination***. You'll get a dialog box asking, "Are you sure you want to set the destination of the selected bookmark to the current location?" Click **Yes** and the bookmark will be updated.

8.5 Renaming

You can also rename bookmarks, if you like. Sometimes you'll want to create bookmarks quickly as you work through a document, so you'll simply be using the keyboard shortcut for creating them (**CMD/CTRL + B**). You'll wind up with a bunch of bookmarks that all have the name "Untitled." Not very helpful, right?

To fix that, simply right-click on the bookmark you want to rename, select *Rename*, type in the bookmark's new name, and hit *Enter* (or *Return*). The bookmark will still point to the same place, but the name will be updated.

8.6 Deleting

Deleting bookmarks becomes necessary periodically, often because the page that the bookmark pointed to has been deleted. You can delete a bookmark by selecting it and then clicking on the trash can icon in the Navigation Pane. Or you can press *Delete*. You can also right-click on the bookmark and choose *Delete*.

You can get rid of several bookmarks at one time. If the bookmarks you want to get rid of are all in a contiguous line, just select the first one, press and hold the **Shift** key, and click the last one. Then delete using any of the methods described.

If the bookmarks are dispersed, just hold down the **CMD/CTRL** key and select the targets by clicking on each one. Once you've selected all the bookmarks you want to delete, use any of the deletion methods we've discussed. The Delete key is probably the fastest and most convenient.

8.7 Wrapping Long Text

If the text of a bookmark's name is long, then all of it might not show up in the Bookmarks view. Sometimes you want bookmarks to display in this manner. Most of the time, I suspect, you would prefer to see all of the text in the bookmark's name. Just go to the ***Bookmarks Pane***, open the ***Options*** menu, and select ***Wrap Long Bookmarks***.

8.8 Splitting Pages by Bookmark

Splitting a PDF by bookmarks is useful when the PDF comprises many different separate documents. Typically, this occurs when you get a batch of paper from a client. That batch represents many individual documents, but the easiest way to scan it is all at once. Then you read through the resulting PDF and create bookmarks to mark the beginning of each document (you'll also want to name the bookmark whatever you want the filename to be when you split up the PDF).

After you've applied bookmarks to the page where each document begins, you're ready to split by bookmarks.

Choose ***Tools > Pages > Split Document***, and you'll be shown a dialog box like Figure 8.7:

Figure 8.7 Splitting a PDF by Bookmarks

Select the option to split by ***Top-level bookmarks*** and then select the ***Out-put Options***. You'll encounter another dialog box, which will present some choices. You'll be asked to decide (1) where you want to save the new files (i.e., the separated documents), and (2) what you want to name those files (see Figure 8.8).

Figure 8.8 Splitting Options

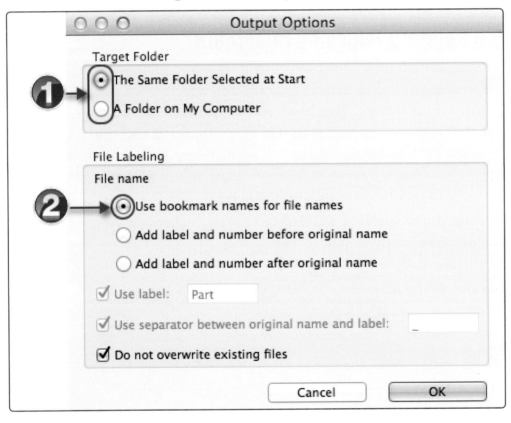

You'll definitely want to use the bookmark names for the filenames, and here's why. You probably have a convention for naming documents; if you don't, then you should. Most lawyers who manage PDFs name their documents by year, month, date, and a description.

For example, you might name a memo from ACME Corporation dated November 21, 1958, as follows: "1958-11-21 ACME Memo." If you follow the convention of using four digits for the year, two digits for the month, and two digits for the date, your documents will automatically sort chronologically. This is why most lawyers use this method.

So, when you're bookmarking a large PDF with the goal of splitting out individual documents as separate PDFs, you'll want to name them using this convention. This way, when the files split out, they'll sort properly. Caveat: you have to make sure each PDF to be split out has a completely unique filename (bookmark name) before the splitting occurs. If the bookmarks/files don't have unique names, Acrobat will choke and disallow the splitting.

The Split Documents feature, along with the Combine feature (which automatically creates bookmarks with the filenames of the incoming documents), means you can split or combine PDFs with the power of bookmarks.

8.9 Setting to Auto-Display Bookmarks

If you've created bookmarks, you'll probably want folks who open the PDF to know that they're there. Most users don't think to look for bookmarks. And frankly, you'll sometimes forget to look yourself if it's a PDF you haven't worked with in a while. So, the best practice is to change the preference for the PDF and set it to display the Bookmarks Pane automatically.

Back in Section 6, we talked about examining PDF documents by selecting *File > Properties* (or using the keyboard shortcut **CMD/CTRL + D**). We didn't cover the **Initial View** options, because it makes more sense to do so here.

Select *Initial View* in the *Document Properties* dialog box and click on the *Navigation tab* drop-down menu, then choose *Bookmarks Panel and Page* (see Figure 8.9).

Figure 8.9 Open Document Properties > Initial View

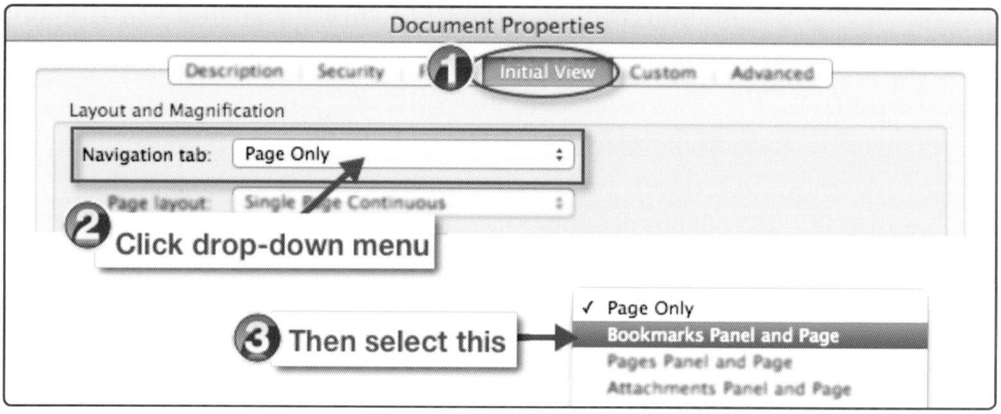

You should make this your standard practice for all PDFs that contain bookmarks. And, incidentally, while you're in the Document Properties dialog box, you can also define how you want the pages to display from the Initial View menus (see Figure 8.10). Any changes you make will override the general display settings in the program used to view the PDF (unless the PDF itself has its own defined page display settings).

Figure 8.10 Setting Initial View Options

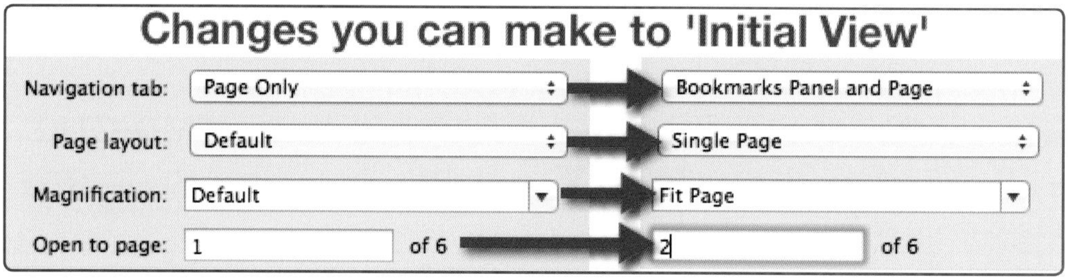

Why would you set a PDF to open to a page other than the first page? Perhaps the title page is simply a cover page that has no useful information, and you want to put the reader on the first page with useful content.

8.10 Changing Properties

You can change the way bookmarks display, if you want. Perhaps you want your bookmarks to appear in **bold**, or *italics*, or ***bold italics***. Maybe you want the bookmarks to display in the color red.

You can change the appearance of a bookmark in that way by opening up the **Properties** for the bookmark.

To do that, you can select the bookmark and then, from the ***Options*** menu, select ***Properties*** from the drop down options. You can also find this choice by right-clicking on the bookmark you want to change. Once you do that you'll get the dialog box shown in Figure 8.11.

Figure 8.11 Changing a Bookmark's Properties

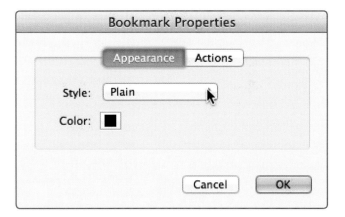

8.10.a Appearance

The **Appearance** tab is where you can change the style of the text (e.g., bold, italics, or bold italics) as well as the color. To change the color, just click on the color that's being displayed, and a drop-down menu of other choices will appear.

8.10.b Actions

Under the **Actions** tab, there are a bunch of options for things that most of you will never want to do. But, to satisfy your curiosity, Figure 8.12 shows the choices you'd be presented with.

Figure 8.12 Setting Bookmark Actions

The main takeaway from looking at Actions options is that you can make a bookmark do a lot more than just navigate around the PDF you have open. You can have it open a different file or even a web link.

8.11 Create from Word Styles

If you use Microsoft Word as your word processor, then you should be familiar with **Styles**. If you're not using Styles, then you're wasting a lot of time and doing formatting the hard way. If you're familiar with Styles, then you should make it a point to use the standard heading styles when you create your briefs and legal memos (you can modify them to suit your preference, if you want).

Figure 8.13 Set Word Styles Prior to PDF Creation

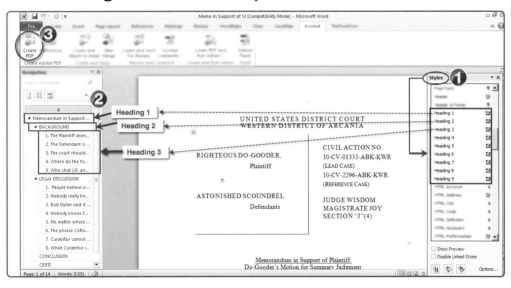

If you use the standard heading styles in Word (modified or unmodified) when you choose ***Create PDF*** from within Word, you'll find that the resulting PDF document will have bookmarks automatically created that are nested in accordance with the heading levels (see Figure 8.13).

Unfortunately, this only works with the Windows version of Word. But, for Mac users here is a simple, inexpensive workaround: download a copy of the free program **OpenOffice** from http://www.openoffice.org/. Then open a DOC or DOCX file that has the heading styles described, and choose **File > Export as PDF** (Make sure **Tagged PDF** and **Export bookmarks** are selected). The resulting PDF will have bookmarks created from style levels described.

If you have trouble opening Open Office after you download it, it's probably because Apple has Mac OS X security set to not allow non-certified applications to open (Open Office is safe, and should be allowed, but it's not). Go to **System Preferences > Security & Privacy > General**. Then change the setting to allow "applications downloaded from" to "anywhere." Run OpenOffice and it should load without any problem (then go back and change the setting back to where it was, because once you've run the program it will keep running even after you change the setting back).

8.12 Bookmarks Need Not Follow Page Order

One thing to bear in mind about bookmarks is that they don't have to follow the order of pages in a PDF. You can drag bookmarks around any way you want; they'll still point to the page they are associated with. That concept is easy to grasp, but most people (me included) forget it—probably because most of the time your bookmarks are sequential, like the pages in the PDF.

Sometimes, however, you might actually want the bookmarks to be arranged in an order completely different from the pages in the PDF. For example, let's say you're in a deposition where documents are being discussed with the deponent. Because you're a power user of PDFs (if you're not now, you will be by the time you finish this book), you're following along by having a large PDF file open—one that contains all of the documents relevant to the case. Whenever your opponent asks about a document, you bookmark it (not even bothering to change the name, since that takes too much time), using the keyboard shortcut that you've dutifully memorized.

When the deposition is over, you'll have a bunch of bookmarks all named "Untitled." You can rename them in the manner we talked about previously. But what about the order of the pages that these bookmarks point to?

Well, the documents referenced by your opponent were probably dispersed throughout your master PDF file, so the bookmarks you created won't be sequential by page number. Do you care? Probably not, and here's why: those bookmarks are in the sequential order of how documents were discussed in the deposition, which might be useful to you.

Now, besides simply bookmarking the documents, you'd probably want to be able to make some quick notes on the PDF pages that were discussed. That way, when you come back later to a page, you'll remember that it was discussed in the deposition and what the focal point of discussion was.

If you were dealing with paper, the way to remind yourself of that would be to highlight key passages and maybe scribble some margin notes. In the world of PDF documents, this activity is called "commenting," and that's what we're going to cover next.

Comments

The commenting tools in Acrobat are all listed on, and are accessible from, the **Comment** menu (refer back to Section 4 for an overview of the Acrobat interface). The Comment tools are divided into **Annotations** and **Drawing Markups** (see Figure 9.1). Once you open the display panels, you'll see icons that show the types of annotation and markup tools you have available.

Figure 9.1 Comment Tools

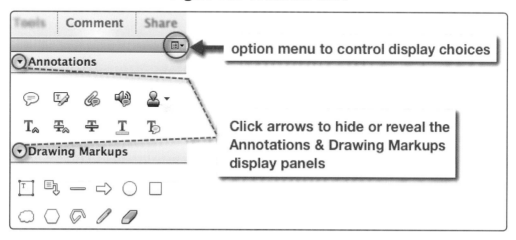

Although there are a lot of options in the Annotations and Drawing Markups panels, if you're like most lawyers, you'll probably rely on three or four at most. Let's take a look at the top choices, which are annotation comments.

9.1 Highlighting

The easiest comment annotation to create is also one you'll be using most often: highlighting. You use the highlighter tool just like you would a yellow highlighter pen. Select the tool and then drag across the text you want to highlight (see Figure 9.2).

Figure 9.2 Highlighter Tool

From there you can continue dragging across areas you want to highlight. If you have trouble getting the highlighting to apply precisely, trying zooming in on the text. If you've forgotten how to zoom, refer back to Section 2 (the shortcut is **CMD/CTRL + Plus** key or **Minus** key).

To remove highlighting (or any annotation or markup, for that matter), just select it and hit ***Delete***. Or right-click on it and choose ***Delete*** from the contextual menu.

Caveat: the PDF must contain searchable text for the highlighter tool to work. You'll know that the PDF isn't text searchable if the tool doesn't work when you try to use it. I'll explain how to convert a PDF into a text-searchable file in Section 11.

9.2 Shortcut for Highlighter Tool

If you enabled single key accelerators (Section 1.4) you can use the letter *U* to quickly switch to the highlighter tool. See the Appendix for the "Single-Key Accelerators Cheat Sheet."

9.3 Adding Text Comments to Highlighting

Ordinarily, when you highlight text, Acrobat simply records that you've flagged some words; it doesn't capture the text that's in those words. But if you followed my advice in Section 1.3, you should have enabled the following preference: **Copy selected text into Highlight, Cross-Out, and Underline comment pop-ups**. If so, then you'll find that Acrobat is also capturing the text that's being highlighted.

If you decide you'd rather create a note regarding that highlighting, you can change the text that Acrobat is associating with the highlighting. Simply double-click on the highlighting, and a pop-up box will appear with the text that was highlighted; select the text and type over it with whatever note you want to create (see Figure 9.3).

Figure 9.3 Editing Text in Pop-Up Comment Box

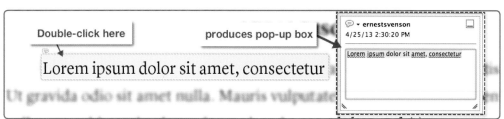

9.4 Changing Comment Properties

If you want the highlighting to be in a different color, you can open up the **Highlight Properties** by right-clicking on the highlighting, and you'll see a dialog box like the one shown in Figure 9.4.

Figure 9.4 Changing Highlight Properties

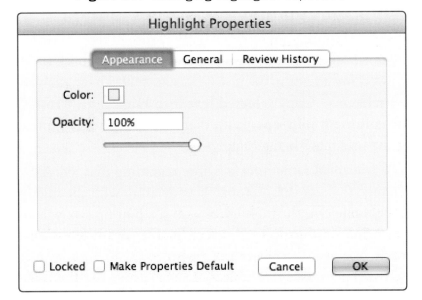

This Properties box is similar to the one we covered when talking about bookmark properties. You can change the highlighting color or its opacity from the **Appearance** tab. You can lock the highlighting so it can't be modified, and you can change the default setting here if you decide you want the changes you make to be the new default for future highlights.

If you click on the **General** tab, you'll see the comment's "author," which will default to whatever you told Acrobat to use when you set up the program (you can change your identity in the program's preferences). You'll also see an option for including a subject, which has defaulted to the type of comment (i.e., "Highlight").

Figure 9.5 Modify the Subject Field

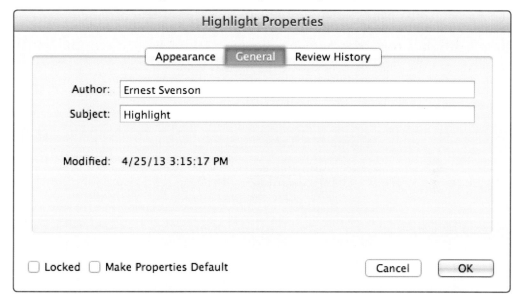

You can change the text in the subject field to anything you want (see Figure 9.5). Some attorneys use this field to match the subject to an issue in their case (e.g., liability, or damages). When you print a comment summary, you'll get to see the subject of each comment. The **Review History** tab is useful if you are collaborating with other folks in making comments to a PDF; it will keep track of changes in the comment's status.

The Properties box works the same way for all of the annotations and highlights that we'll talk about next.

9.5 Sticky Notes

The next most commonly used annotation is sticky notes. These look like little yellow speech bubbles and are useful for making comments of the sort that you'd write on a yellow sticky note on a hard-copy document. But whereas paper notes are limited by the size of the sticky, these comments can contain a lot of text—probably more than you'd ever type in.

To create a sticky note, you have several options. You can select it from the **Annotations** panel, or—if you value efficiency—you can use the keyboard shortcut **CMD/CTRL + 6**. If you have enabled single-key accelerators, you can simply press the *S* key. Having switched to the sticky-note tool using one of those methods, just click in the area of the PDF where you want the note to go (see Figure 9.6).

Figure 9.6 Creating Sticky Notes

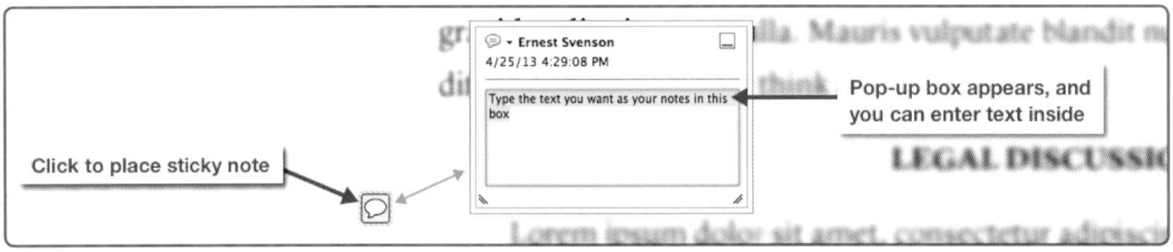

A pop-up box will appear (not necessarily next to where you clicked), and you'll be able to enter text. You can drag the pop-up box to where you prefer it to be, and you can drag the sticky note around as well. Once you're finished entering text, you can click in the top right corner of the pop-up box or hit the *Escape* key to dismiss the box quickly.

9.6 Restore Deleted Sticky Note

If you accidentally delete a sticky note, you can restore it by selecting *Edit > Undo*. You can keep selecting Undo to restore more deletions or changes.

9.7 Callout Text Box

The callout text box is a cross between the sticky note and the highlighter. If you select this tool and then drag across some text, it will highlight the text and then open a pop-up box like the sticky note, which will allow you to enter comments. But we've already seen that we can do the same thing by double-clicking on the highlighted text after we've selected it with the highlighter tool.

The callout text box is most useful if you have enabled the preference **Copy selected text into Highlight, Cross-Out, and Underline comment pop-ups** and want a tool from time to time that will let you highlight but not copy the selected text.

9.8 Underlining and Boxes

In the **Drawing Markups** panel, there are several tools that allow you to draw circles, arrows, lines, boxes, and so forth. Typically, lawyers need only a few basic tools to mark up a PDF. The line tool is good for creating underlines for emphasis; the box tool is good for circumscribing important areas; the arrow tool is good for pointing at things.

All of these tools are easy to figure out. It's worth mentioning that holding down the Shift key as you draw the shapes will have the following effects: it will ensure that the lines you draw are restrained to be completely level across the page; it will make boxes square instead of rectangular (if you want rectangles, don't hold down the Shift key); and it will create circles instead of ellipses (don't use the Shift key if you want an ellipsis).

9.9 Text Annotations

Lawyers who collaborate in creating documents (typically, transactional lawyers) often use Microsoft Word with the "track changes" feature turned on. However, sometimes lawyers want to collaborate in drafting a document, but not share the underlying word processing file. In that case, they should consider using the text annotation tools in Acrobat.

Those tools are found under ***Comment > Annotations***. The main choices are: **insert text**, **replace text**, **strikethrough**, and **underline**, as shown in Figure 9.7.

Figure 9.7 Text Annotation Markup Tools

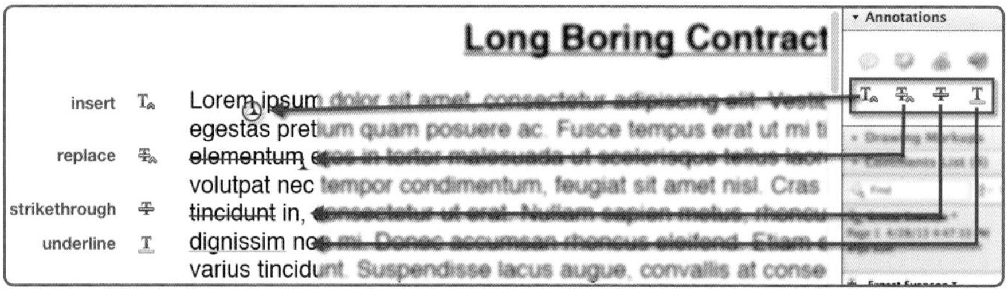

For these tools to work, the document has to be a text PDF, or be made into a text selectable PDF using the OCR tool described in Section 11. Typically, if you try to select text in an image PDF (i.e., one that was created by scanning paper) you'll see a dialog box like the one in Figure 9.8, which offers to run character analysis (which some folks call "OCR").

Figure 9.8 Warning: PDF Is Not Text-Selectable

Usually, you'll want to let Acrobat run the character analysis. (This is the same as the Recognize Text function.) After it does, you'll be able to select text and highlight it.

9.10 Reviewing Comments

Once you've made a bunch of comments in a PDF, you'll probably want to be able to review them. However, there is no way to automatically tell Acrobat to open up the comments review list for a PDF that has comments. So, you'll just have to remember to check that list yourself (of course, you'll likely notice the comments as you scroll through the PDF).

Figure 9.9 Comments List

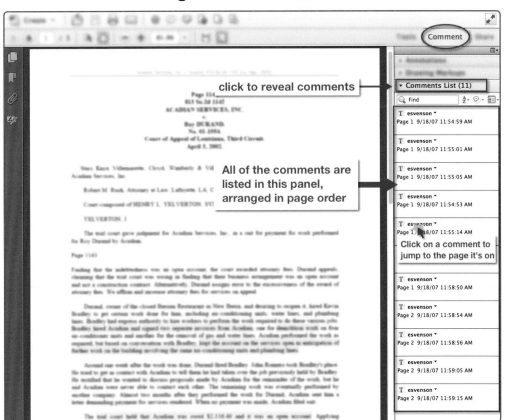

To review comments, open the ***Comment*** menu and click on ***Comments List***, as shown in Figure 9.9. You probably noticed the number 11 in parentheses. This is indicates that there are eleven comments in the PDF.

Each comment shows the author, the page on which the comment exists, and the date and time of its creation. To quickly jump to a particular comment, simply click on its summary, and you'll immediately go to the page in the PDF where the comment is located.

9.11 Deleting Several Comments at Once

I've explained how to delete comments one at a time, but what if you want to delete several at a time? Simple. Just open the Comments List (see Figure 9.9), and cherry-pick the ones you want to delete by selecting them. To select a bunch that are next to each other, click on the first one, hold the ***Shift*** key, and click on the last one. Then hit ***Delete***.

To choose several that aren't contiguous, hold down the **CMD/CTRL** key and select the comments you want to delete. When you're done selecting, release the **CMD/CTRL** key and then hit ***Delete***.

General Text Editing

As I said in the introduction, PDF files are akin to "digital paper" in that they represent a paper document, which in some instances will be marked up with comments. But you can add text to a PDF and even edit the text displayed in a PDF. Not that Acrobat is going to replace your word processor; practically speaking, the text in PDF files is editable only up to a point. Also, you can't edit text in a PDF that you scanned and then ran the Recognize Text function (Section 11).

If a PDF document has blank areas in which you want to place text, or if it is a scanned copy of a paper form, you can type text into the PDF just as if you were using a typewriter. The process of adding or editing text is slightly different in Acrobat editions X and XI. The names of the tools also differ a bit, but the main change has been that editing text gets easier and more powerful in each edition.

Most lawyers will find Acrobat's text-editing tools useful for small jobs. For example, if you've made a mistake in the date of a certificate of service in a PDF you're about to electronically file, you don't have to go back to your word processor to fix it; you can use Acrobat to edit the date text.

We will talk about how text editing is done in each version of Acrobat. I'll focus first on Acrobat XI. If you have Acrobat X, skip Section 10.1.

10.1 Acrobat XI Text Editing

Here's how text editing works in Acrobat XI. Open ***Tools > Content Editing***, and you'll see several choices as shown in Figure 10.1.

Figure 10.1 Text Editing in Acrobat XI

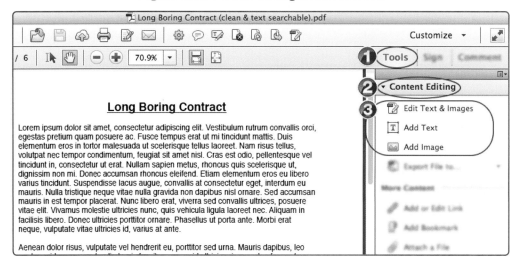

Edit Text & Images will allow you to replace text in an existing document. You can use **Add Text** to enter text in a new area of the PDF where no text exists; many legal professionals use this tool to add text to PDF forms that aren't fillable (e.g., the forms were simply scanned in from the paper version). This tool was formerly called **Typewriter**.

To use the **Edit Text & Images** tool, you must have a PDF that was created from a text-based program, such as a word processor, or was made searchable through the OCR method that will be discussed in Section 11. Assuming you have searchable (or selectable) text, the process is simple: Click on ***Edit Text & Images*** and then double-click the word (or drag across the several words) to be edited, as shown in Figure 10.2.

Figure 10.2 Select Text to Edit

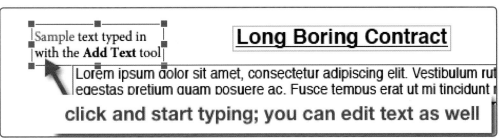

Note the red circles around the markers showing that the entire paragraph is an editable area. It used to be that you could make minor edits to only a few words at most. In Acrobat XI, you can theoretically replace an entire paragraph, if you want.

Using the **Add Text** tool is just as simple: select the tool and place your cursor where you want to enter text (see Figure 10.3).

Figure 10.3 Adding Text

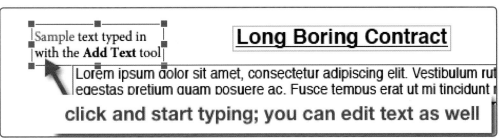

You can stretch the text out by dragging one of the points on the bounding box, and you can edit the text as well. To edit, just use the *Format* palette that appears in the *Task Pane* and looks like the image in Figure 10.4.

The **Format** palette allows you to change the font type, color, and size. You can also add bold, italics, and underlining, and change the justification. You can even add superscript or subscript. This same palette allows you to edit graphics, including cropping and rotation.

Acrobat XI's editing abilities are amazingly powerful.

Figure 10.4 Format Palatte

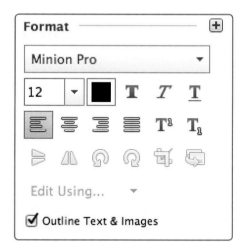

10.2 Acrobat X Text Editing

The text-editing abilities of Acrobat X are more limited than Acrobat XI, but the process of selecting the tools is pretty much the same. Open **Tools > Content** (called **Content Editing** in Acrobat XI), and you'll see several choices (see Figure 10.5).

Figure 10.5 Text Editing in Acrobat X

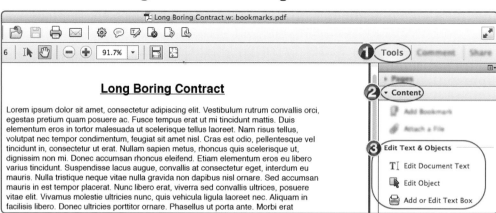

Edit Document Text will allow you to replace text in an existing document. **Add or Edit Text Box** is mostly used for adding text to a new area of the PDF where no text exists; many legal professionals use this tool to add text to PDF forms that aren't fillable (e.g., the forms were simply scanned in from the paper version). This was formerly the **Typewriter** tool.

Note: To use these tools, you must have a PDF that was created from a text-based program, such as a word processor. Again, you can't edit text that was made searchable through the Recognize Text method that will be discussed in Section 11.

Select *Edit Document Text* and then simply drag across the word or words to be edited, as shown in Figure 10.6.

Figure 10.6 Select Text to Edit

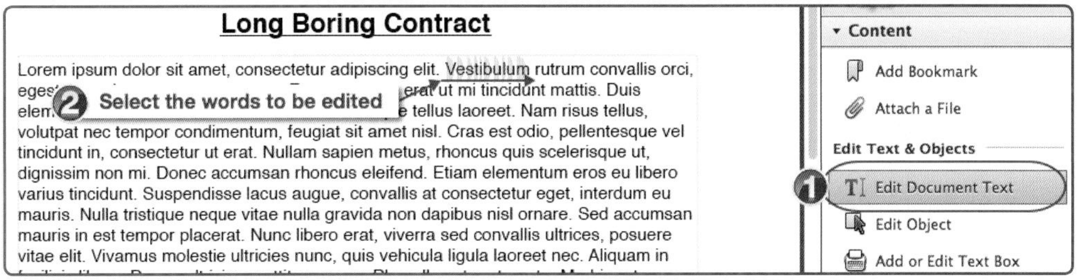

There is a limit to how much editing you can do. And if you read the prior section on Acrobat XI, you'll appreciate the vast difference. But it's just as simple to edit the text in Acrobat X.

Using the Add or Edit Text Box tool is also easy. Just select the tool and place your cursor where you want to enter text. You'll get a floating toolbar like the one shown in Figure 10.7, from which you can choose different fonts, font colors, justification, and line spacing.

Figure 10.7 Typewriter Toolbar

Notice that the word *Typewriter* appears in the header of the toolbar. Many lawyers still call this the Typewriter tool (so if you hear someone refer to it by its old name, don't get confused).

After you've typed in the text, you can move it around. Just click on the text you typed and you'll see a bounding box, as shown in Figure 10.8.

Figure 10.8 Typewriter Tool in Action

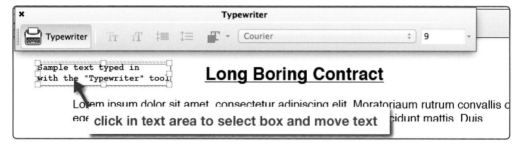

You can drag the box around to where you want it, or you can stretch the text out by dragging on one of the points at the left or right end of the box. Obviously, you can also edit the text you typed.

Recognize Text Function (OCR)

For a user to be able to select text or search for text in a PDF, the document has to be "text searchable." If you create a PDF by exporting a file from a word processing program, then it almost certainly will be text searchable. If you create a PDF by using a scanner or some other means, you'll probably have to make it text searchable.

While Adobe calls this function **Recognize Text,** you'll hear many people refer to this process as OCR.

11.1 What Is OCR and How Does It Work?

The term OCR (optical character recognition) comes from the process by which the computer makes the text searchable. Basically, when you use OCR on a document, your computer software (in this case, Acrobat) examines every cluster of pixels to see if it's in the shape of a letter in the Western alphabet. If the software finds a cluster that looks like the letter *a*, it assigns that value. And it figures out that clusters of letters separated by spaces are words.

In the beginning, OCR took a long time and was very error prone. As computers have gotten more powerful and the software algorithms more refined, the OCR process has become pretty fast and much more accurate. Acrobat XI has a robust and reliable OCR function (Recognize Text).

Some of you may remember OCR being used in the early days mostly as a way of capturing text in a document so that it wouldn't have to be retyped; instead, it could be quickly imported into a word processor for efficient editing.

And you probably remember that if you used OCR on a document of poor quality, it might convert "The quick brown fox jumps over the lazy dog" to something like "The 9uick br0wn f()x j0mps owr th3 l@zy d0g." And you'd see this problem right away since you were viewing the result in a word processing program.

In Acrobat, you run Recognize Text not to edit the text but to search it, or to be able to highlight it. Hence, the document image will be preserved and not supplanted by the recognized text.

11.2 Optimal Scanner Settings

If you're scanning documents that will require OCR, you should scan in at the best settings to ensure maximum OCR accuracy. Here are some of the optimal settings for most situations:

- Scan in black and white. (If you need the document to be in color, choose that, but the file size will be much bigger.)
- Scan at 300 dpi (dots per inch) if possible (600 is better, but *not less than 300 dpi*). The higher the dpi setting, the better image quality, which will increase the accuracy of text recognition when doing OCR.

Obviously, you can't control the quality of a scanned PDF that was given to you; in that case, you have to make do with what you've got.

11.3 How to Use "Recognize Text"

Let's begin by demonstrating Recognize Text with settings that are best for most lawyers. First, choose **_Recognize Text_** from the **_Tools_** menu (see Figure 11.1).

Then, specify if you want to perform the operation on an open file (**In This File**) or on several files, which need not be open (**In Multiple Files**).

Figure 11.1 Recognize Text

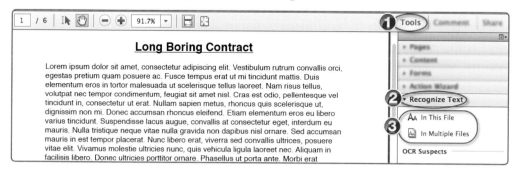

After you select the file(s) on which to perform the operation, you'll see a dialog box like the one in Figure 11.2.

You can choose to perform the operation on all pages, just the current page, or a range of pages. You'll also be shown what settings will be used. The first time you use Acrobat to recognize text, you'll want to click the ***Edit*** button and make some adjustments. You'll see a dialog box like the one in Figure 11.3.

Figure 11.2 Options for Recognize Text

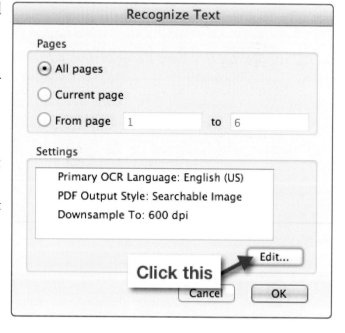

Figure 11.3 Set to Searchable Image (Exact)

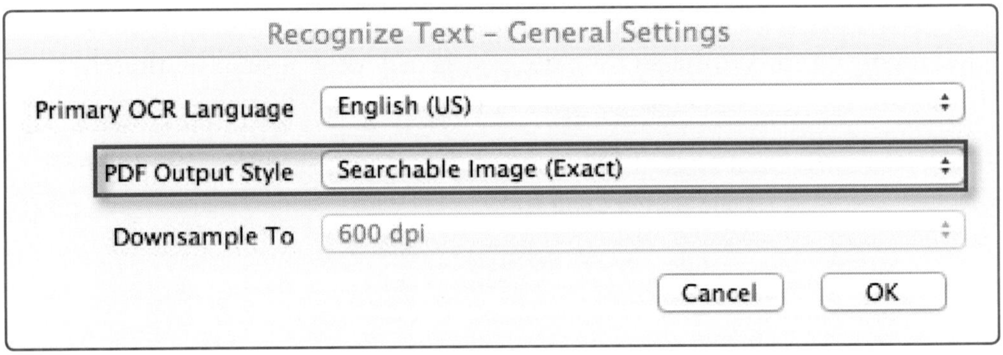

Choosing ***Searchable Image (Exact)*** will produce the highest-quality image; most legal professionals want the greatest fidelity and flexibility, so that's usually the safest and best option.

During the OCR process, you may receive notices that Acrobat was not sure about a word or two in the document. After the process is complete, you have the option to find suspect words and correct them. To do so, choose ***Tools > Text Recognition > Find First Suspect*** (or ***Find All Suspects***). You will then be able to find and correct words so that the searchable text accurately reflects the original text.

When you run Recognize Text on multiple files at once, you won't get error notices, which is good because you don't want the process to stop and wait for you to acknowledge potential errors. You can still go find and correct them afterward.

Once you've run the Recognize Text function, just click ***Save*** (or ***Save As***, if you want to keep the original file).

POWER TIP

The Recognize Text process straightens pages.

One benefit of running the Recognize Text function is that any pages that were scanned in crooked will be straightened. This process is called "deskewing" and is done so that the text is as level as possible, thereby increasing OCR accuracy.

If you have PDFs that are crooked but don't need OCR, you can use the **Optimize Scanned PDF** tool (*Tools > Document Processing > Optimize Scanned PDF*).

11.4 When You Shouldn't Use "Recognize Text"

Lawyers have a tendency to think that if a little OCR is good, then more will always be better. Here are some reasons why you might *not* want to OCR certain files:

- OCR often (but not always) makes the file size bigger.
- OCR takes extra time to do, and then you have to check for quality. In any event, when you OCR case documents you should always keep a backup set in non-OCR format.

Many PDF-savvy attorneys have made it a standard practice *not* to OCR correspondence, pleadings, or anything other than their case documents. But, as file storage costs decrease and OCR becomes faster and easier, other attorneys are finding that it's simpler just to OCR everything.

Stamps

Stamps are a type of annotation, but they aren't typically used for commenting. Most of the stamps that come with Acrobat are designed for general business purposes. Some are useful for lawyers, too.

12.1 Standard, Dynamic, and Custom Stamps

The best way to get a sense of what stamps are available is to poke around the options that are shown when you access the stamp tool, which you do by opening the ***Comment*** menu, selecting ***Annotations,*** and clicking on the stamp icon (you can also add the stamp tool to the toolbar and then access it from there).

As you can see in Figure 12.1, there are at least three categories of stamps. The first two are **Standard Business** and **Dynamic** (which means that the stamp will automatically add information, such as the author and date and time of stamping).

Figure 12.1 Examples of PDF Stamps

Standard Business Stamps —

"Dynamic" Stamps —

Custom Exhibit Stamps —

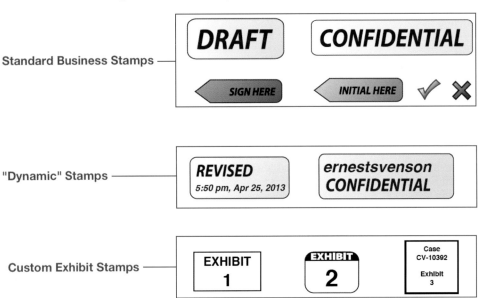

Using the preloaded stamps is easy. Just pick the stamp you want to use and click in the area where you want it to appear. Make it smaller or larger by grabbing one of points on the bounding box, as shown in Figure 12.2.

Figure 12.2 Change Stamp Size

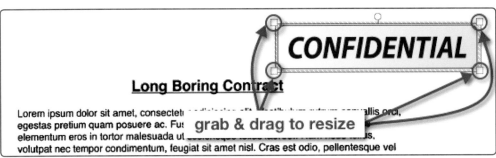

The third type of stamp is one that you create yourself or import—the **custom stamp**. A custom stamp needs a graphic or custom artwork that will become the stamp. The graphic image should be in a common format, such as JPG or PNG. If you want text to go with the image, you can set that up using a program like Microsoft Word or PowerPoint.

Once you've got the graphic/text image set up, you can import it as follows: ***Comment > Annotations > stamp icon > Custom Stamps > Create Custom Stamp***. You'll then be asked to browse for the file you want to use as the custom stamp. Once you have it loaded in, you'll get a dialog box like Figure 12.3.

Figure 12.3 Organizing Stamps

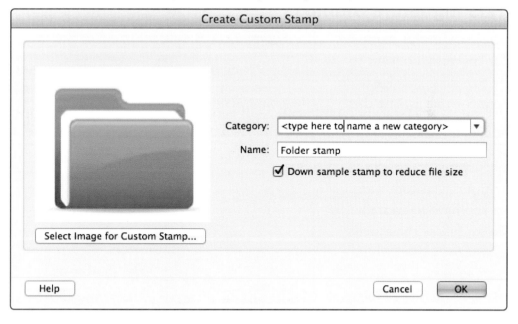

Type in the name of the stamp. If it belongs to a group of stamps you're just now starting to use, then type in a new category name too. For example, I put all my signature stamps in a category called "Signatures," and all my exhibit stamps in a group with the name "Exhibit Stamps."

12.2 Custom Exhibit Stamp

Among lawyers, a popular custom stamp is the exhibit stamp. The customization process not only lets you create a stamp that says "Exhibit" but also makes it easy to add the exhibit numbers or letters as you use the stamp. To find out more about these kinds of stamps search the web using this phrase: "custom PDF exhibit stamp."

12.3 Signature Stamps

The most useful stamp for lawyers who want to be paperless is a signature stamp—that is, one that lets you stamp a copy of your signature on a PDF document. A signature stamp is a custom stamp, so you have to create it. To do so, follow these steps: *Comment > Annotations > stamp icon > Custom Stamps > Create Custom Stamp* (see Figure 12.4).

Figure 12.4 Create a Signature Stamp

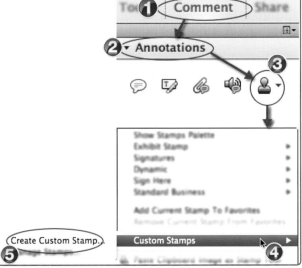

If you have scanned your signature and saved it as a graphic file (JPG or PNG), you can import it as a custom stamp. Just browse for it, and when you see the dialog box showing your signature graphic loaded in, click *OK* (see Figure 12.5).

The graphic will appear in the group you assigned to it when you imported it. It's probably a good idea to create a stamp group called "Signatures" and put it in there. You should also have a graphic of your initials, since often you'll be asked to initial a document as well.

Figure 12.5 Browse for Image of Signature

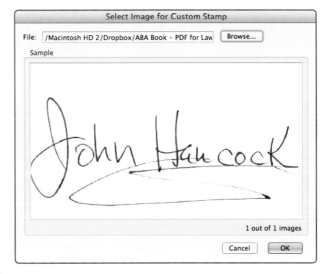

12.4 Transparent Signature Stamps Are Best

The best kind of signature stamp is one that has a transparent background. When you stamp it near text, it will look like you signed on top of the text, which makes the recipient less likely to question the signature's validity. Figure 12.6 shows examples of two signature stamps: one with a white background (undesirable) and one with a transparent background (desirable).

Figure 12.6 Non-transparent versus Transparent Signatures

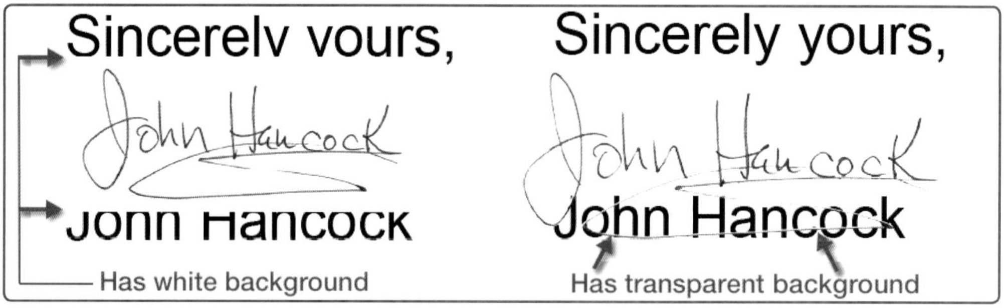

The process by which you get rid of the background isn't too difficult, but it's tricky for folks who aren't comfortable with Adobe Photoshop or Photoshop Elements (if you're tech-savvy and super-frugal, you can use the free image-editing program called **Gimp**). For most people, the simplest way is to use Microsoft Word. Rick Borstein explains how in this blog post at http://adobe.ly/AmWMKn.

12.5 Flattening Your Stamped PDFs

Once you've stamped a document with your signature, you'll need to "flatten" the PDF so that the signature is permanently affixed. You do this not to keep people from *getting* your signature (anyone who knows how to use Photoshop can easily get a screen capture of your signature from a PDF or a hard-copy letter and create a signature stamp), but to keep a recipient of the PDF from accidentally printing it without the markups, resulting in a document that doesn't have your signature showing. One way to flatten a PDF is by using **Action Wizard**—a feature that only exists in Acrobat Professional.

Action Wizard is like a macro. It can perform a sequence on a PDF or add a feature to Acrobat quickly, without the need for you to know a lot of technical code. If you have a PDF that has the flattening action installed, you simply open the PDF and run the action once, and it will be permanently installed in your copy of Acrobat. See Figure 12.7.

Figure 12.7 Flattening Action

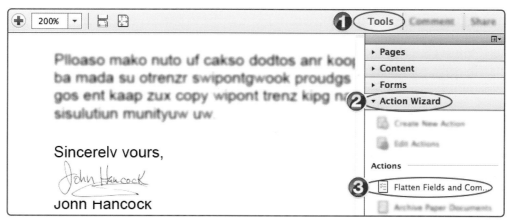

The action that's needed to create flattening in Acrobat X is different from the one required for Acrobat XI, but both are available for download at www.pdfforlawyers.com/resources/. (Look for "Flattening Actions for Acrobat X and Acrobat XI.")

Installing a flattening action can seem intimidating to many folks, so here's a simple work-around for those of you with PCs. After applying a signature stamp (or other annotation) that you want to flatten, simply use the "print to PDF" option described in Section 5.2. Unfortunately, you can't "print to PDF" if you're using a Mac.

12.6 PDF Signatures on Mobile Devices

Interestingly, it's easier to sign a PDF on an iPad or Android tablet than on a desktop computer. The touch screen makes it simple to scrawl your signature using your finger or a stylus. The free Adobe Reader app (available on iOS or Android) allows you to tap and hold to get a signature tool, which you can easily use to sign a PDF document. After signing, you simply e-mail it to the appropriate recipient, who will receive a PDF that has automatically been flattened.

So, if you have an iPad or Android tablet, this is probably the easiest way to sign a PDF document.

Digital Signatures

The signature stamps that we just created are properly termed "electronic signatures." A true digital signature, on the other hand, carries more weight. A digital signature is like a fingerprint that ensures the authenticity of the person(s) signing a PDF. Acrobat can create and authenticate digital signatures.

However, it should be emphasized—truly *emphasized*—that 99 percent of the time the simple signature stamp will suffice. In fact, if you try to use a true digital signature in situations where the recipient isn't versed in using them, the outcome will likely be that your signature will be questioned and possibly rejected.

You also need to be aware that the process of creating digital signatures varies between Acrobat X and Acrobat XI. The process is easier in Acrobat XI and less likely to result in raised eyebrows, mostly because it's integrated with Adobe's online **EchoSign** service.

Bottom line: don't obsess about creating true digital signatures. Usually they're not necessary. And trying to use them with people who don't understand how to use them (i.e., most people) just creates unnecessary chaos and confusion.

Bates Numbering

Bates numbering has been a staple process for legal professionals for many years now. Originally, Bates numbers were affixed to paper documents using a handheld stamping machine created by the Bates Manufacturing Company. The process was noisy and prone to error: it was easy to miss a page, which then required the stamper to go back and create a special intervening number.

More recently, the Bates stamp was supplanted by word processing methods, using macros, that generated a series of Bates labels that could then be peeled off and stuck to the pages of a document. This method was less noisy, but still tedious and error prone.

The fastest and most reliable way to put Bates numbers on documents is to scan the documents and then let a computer handle the task. First and most important: make a copy of the PDF(s) before you start to do Bates stamping.

14.1 Adding Bates Numbers with Acrobat

Adobe Acrobat can stamp a single PDF or a batch of PDFs—quickly, reliably, and with several useful options. The process is as follows: ***Tools***

> *Pages* > *Bates Numbering* > *Add Bates Numbering*. You'll be asked to designate the files or folders that you want to perform the operation on, and then you'll get a dialog box (shown in Figure 14.1) from which you can make several choices, beginning with font style, font size, font color, and placement of the Bates numbers.

Figure 14.1 Bates Numbering Options

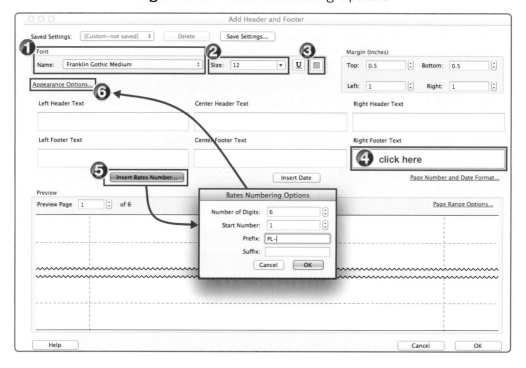

Acrobat defaults to Arial font, 8 point, black. In his excellent book *Typography for Lawyers*, Matthew Butterick recommends avoiding Arial because it's hard to read (the 8-point size is definitely too small). He recommends 12-point font, preferably something like Franklin Gothic Medium. Choosing a red or orange font ensures that the Bates number will stand out. Those are the choices shown in Figure 14.2, in numbers 1, 2, and 3.

After you choose the font and its size and color, you need to specify where you want the Bates number to appear. Most lawyers seem to prefer the lower right-hand side of the page. If that's your preference, click in the ***Right Footer Text*** box (4) and then click ***Insert Bates Number*** (5), which will cause a small dialog box to pop up, allowing you to choose the number of digits you want your Bates numbers to have. You will also be allowed to specify the start number, a prefix (such as *PL* for plaintiff), and a suffix, if you like.

Before you click OK, you might want to do one more thing, especially if the PDFs you're stamping have images or other content in the area where the stamps will go. In that situation, the Bates numbers might not be visible, and that would be bad. To avoid that problem, click on the blue link that says ***Appearance Options***, and you'll get the following pop-up box.

Figure 14.2 Shrink Document Option

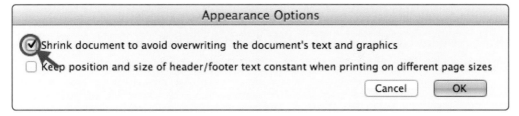

Select the option checked in Figure 14.2. Then click ***OK*** and you're almost ready. If you like this setting and intend to use it again in the future, you'll want to save it by clicking ***Save Settings*** at the top of the Bates numbering dialog box and then give the style a name (see Figure 14.3).

Figure 14.3 Save Preferred Settings

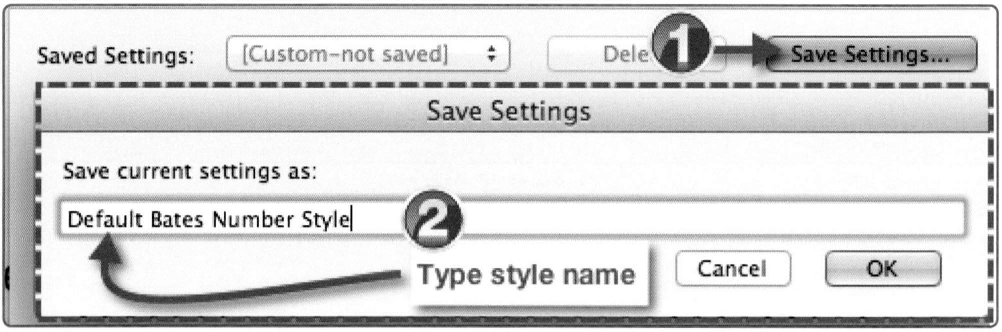

Click **OK** to save the setting and then click **OK** to perform the Bates numbering. The process is pretty quick, even if you have hundreds of pages in the PDF. If you want to preserve the old file, you can save the Bates-stamped version as a new file.

14.2 Deleting Bates Numbers

If you made a mistake or later want to remove the Bates numbers, you can reverse the process easily by selecting **Tools > Pages > Bates Numbering > Remove**. Caveat: obviously, you can only remove Bates numbers that *you've* added. If you receive documents with Bates numbers put in by someone else, you can't use this process to remove those numbers.

Redaction

Lawyers frequently deal with sensitive information and often have to produce documents that obscure that sensitive information. Litigators, especially, are used to the notion of redacting confidential information. Acrobat has had a redaction function since version 8. The function is well developed in Acrobat XI, to the point where it probably has all the features and robustness that any lawyer would need.

Some lawyers have made the mistake of attempting to cover up sensitive information by using a **Drawing Markup** tool, such as a rectangle with solid fill. They place the solid rectangle over the sensitive area and then produce the PDF, thinking that no one will ever be able to discover the "hidden" information. If you read a news story about a law firm having "redaction failure," you can be sure that this is what happened; someone used the wrong tool to perform redaction.

15.1 Proper Redaction

The proper way (indeed, the *only* way) to do redaction is with the redaction tool. The redaction function in Acrobat doesn't merely cover up text or images; it replaces the selected areas pixel-for-pixel with the redaction fill you specify.

Here's how it works: from the ***Tools*** menu, select ***Protection*** and you'll find several commands related to redaction (see Figure 15.1).

Begin by selecting ***Mark for Redaction*** and then drag across the area of the page that you want to obscure. If the area you want to redact is searchable text, you'll see the "selection" cursor. If the area is not text searchable, you'll see a "crosshair" cursor. After you drag across the area to be marked, you'll see the default redaction fill, which will probably look something like Figure 15.2.

Figure 15.1 Redaction Commands

Figure 15.2 Redaction Designated (but Not Applied)

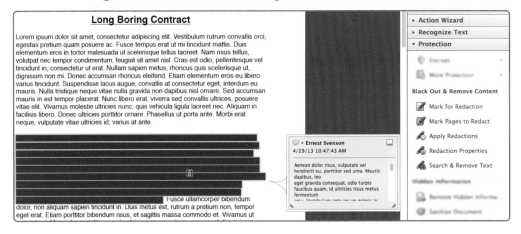

The area may be marked in black in your version of Acrobat; whatever you see is the default. You'll also notice that a pop-up window displays the text that has been marked for redaction. When you move your mouse away from the redacted area, it will return to normal view—making it impossible to tell that you marked it for redaction.

If you make a mistake in selecting an area to be redacted, simply choose *Edit > Undo* (or use the keyboard shortcut **CMD/CTRL + Z**).

Continue going through the document, designating areas to be redacted. You can also select entire pages: from *Tools > Protection*, choose *Mark Pages to Redact* and then designate which pages you want to obscure.

When you're done, you can either choose *Apply Redactions* or save the PDF and apply the redactions later. One reason you might want to wait is so another lawyer can review the proposed changes to confirm that they're appropriate.

When you try to save a PDF with designated redactions that have not yet been applied, you'll get a warning like the one in Figure 15.3.

Figure 15.3 Warning: Redaction Not Yet Applied

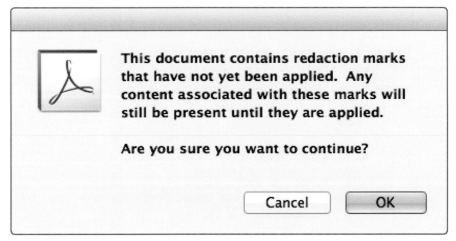

Acrobat isn't telling you that you aren't *allowed* to save without applying the redactions; it's simply warning you that it's *dangerous* (because
you might forget to apply them later and accidentally produce the PDF
without redactions being applied).

You should probably also save a copy of the original PDF as part of
your routine workflow. You'll need a copy of the unmarked version if your
claim of privilege is later deemed improper.

15.2 Redaction Review

So, let's assume you're the senior lawyer who wants to review the proposed
redactions. What's the best way to do that? Open the document, then go
to the *Comment* menu and select *Comments List*, at which point something like Figure 15.4 will be displayed.

Figure 15.4 Review Designated Redactions in Comment List

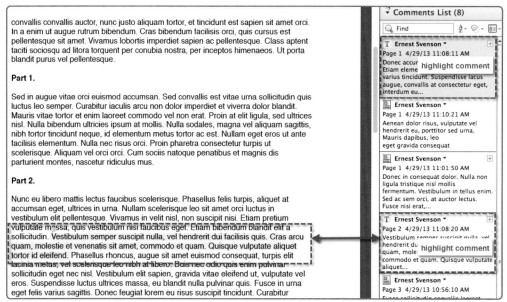

Figure 15.5 Filter Comments

Figure 15.6 Filter for Redaction Comments Only

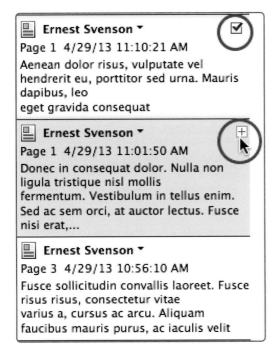

Notice that the Comments List includes all types of comments, including the yellow highlighting. You'll need to filter the Comments List to include only the redaction comments. The way to do that is to select the *Filter comments* option, as shown in Figure 15.5.

After that, choose *Type > Redact* and then you'll see only redaction-type comments. And from there you can go through and check off the ones that you deem appropriate. You won't see a check box unless you click on the plus sign; after that, you'll be able to check the box. See Figure 15.6 for an example.

When you're done, you can save the PDF with your review comments (Acrobat will warn you that the redactions have not been applied). You can also filter for the unchecked redactions—the ones you don't want to apply. Select the *Filter comments* option (as shown in Figure 15.5) and choose

Checked > Unchecked. Now you'll see only the proposed redactions that you've concluded should *not* be applied. To delete the redaction marks, select all the displayed comments and hit *Delete*.

A key takeaway here is that you can make global changes to redactions from the Comments List. One kind of global change you might want to make is to the properties associated with the redaction marks you've made. Let's say you decide that, instead of red solid fill, you want the redaction marks to say "Redacted" across any area you've redacted. We'll discuss how to change redaction properties in Section 15.4.

15.3 Create Review Summaries

If you want to create a printout (or PDF) summary of all the comments to send for someone else's review, you can easily do that. Just click the small *Options* menu on the far right of the Comments List, as shown in Figure 15.7.

Select *Create Comment Summary* and you'll see a dialog box with options for how the summary should look and what it should include (see Figure 15.8).

Figure 15.7 Create Comment Summary

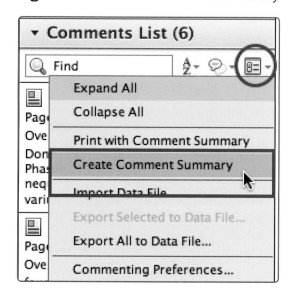

Figure 15.8 Options for Comment Summary

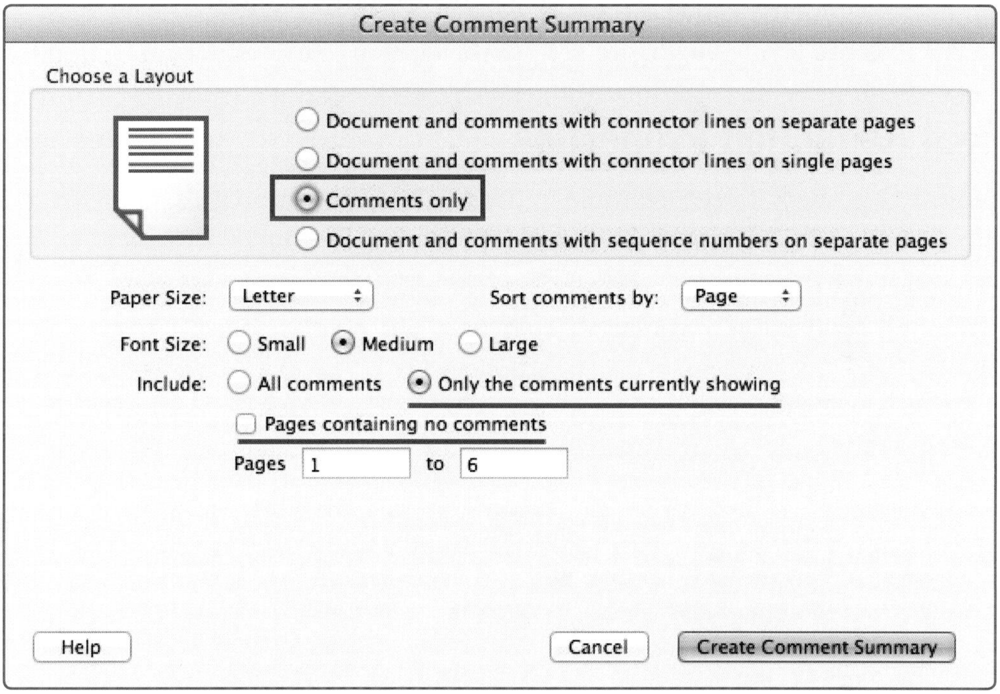

My recommendations are as follows: first, choose **_Comments only_**. Then, if you've filtered the comments, you'll probably want to include only the ones that you're focused on. If so, select **_Only the comments currently showing_**. Finally, you probably don't want to include pages that have no comments, so do not check the box next to **Pages containing no comments**.

POWER TIP

Comment filtering works for any kind of comment.

This type of comment filtering and use of check boxes is helpful for any kind of comment review—not just redactions.

15.4 Redaction Properties

Now, let's go back to the example in Section 15.2 of a global change. What is the best way to change redaction marks to say "Redacted" instead of being red solid fill? You could go through and right-click on each area that you marked for redaction and make the changes one by one. But the more

Figure 15.9 Redaction Properties

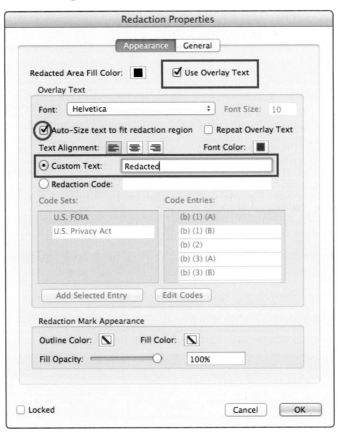

efficient way is to go to the ***Comments List***, select all the redaction marks you want to apply the change to, right-click there, and choose ***Properties***. Then you'll see very comprehensive dialog box shown in Figure 15.9.

Choose ***Use Overlay Text***, check ***Auto-Size text to fit redaction region***, and then type in your ***Custom Text***. In addition, you have the option to change the fill color and opacity. Notice that you can also use redaction codes; Acrobat comes preloaded with a set of codes for the Freedom of Information Act and the U.S. Privacy Act. You can even create your own set of codes by selecting the ***Edit Codes*** button.

In short, there are many options that you can use to make redactions work exactly like you want them to. For more information on redacting with Acrobat, see Rick Borstein's *Acrobat for Legal Professionals* blog at http://blogs. adobe.com/acrolaw/category/redaction/.

15.5 Search and Redact

Acrobat has the ability to let you search for phrases that need to be redacted, as well as patterns such as phone numbers, credit cards, e-mail addresses, dates, or social security numbers. To use this feature, choose ***Tools > Protection > Search & Remove Text*** (see Figure 15.10).

After selecting **Search & Remove Text**, you'll get a dialog box on the left-hand side that looks like the search dialog box we'll be covering in Section 17. Select what you want to search for: **Single word or phrase**, **Multiple words or phrase**, or **Patterns**. If you choose Patterns,

Figure 15.10
Search and Remove Text

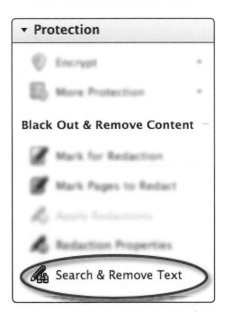

you'll see the options for searching for phone numbers, credit cards, e-mail addresses, dates, or social security numbers (see Figure 15.11).

Figure 15.11 Search Options

You aren't limited to searching in the PDF you currently have open; you can search other PDFs by designating a folder that you want to search and redact. Once you initiate the search, you'll be presented with familiar options for applying redactions and then accepting them.

Caveat: although pattern matching is convenient for quickly identifying data to be scrubbed, it is *not perfect*. In other words, there is no substitute for reviewing a document the old-fashioned way: by reading every page closely.

Metadata Removal

Metadata seems to confuse a lot of people, including lawyers. Although this may not be an "official definition," the best way to conceptualize metadata is to think of it as "hidden data." Metadata isn't necessarily bad; it may be completely innocuous. But unless you dig it up to see what it contains, you won't know.

16.1 How to Remove Metadata

Since most people don't know how to dig for metadata in a PDF file, Adobe has made it easy to find and delete metadata. From the ***Tools*** menu, select ***Protection > Remove Hidden Information*** (see Figure 16.1).

Figure 16.1 Deleting Metadata

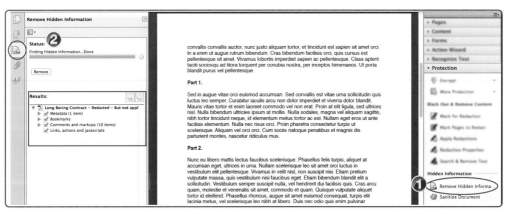

When you click on ***Remove Hidden Information***, a panel will open on the left-hand side of the document and show a status bar indicating when the document scan is complete. It will also display a list of the types of "hidden information" Acrobat found. Interestingly, Acrobat considers any kind of comment, annotation, or bookmark to be hidden information. But you can deselect the types that you want to keep in the document by checking the boxes next to them.

You can get more information about what kind of metadata is present in the PDF by clicking on the expansion arrow next to the Metadata designation in the list. And then you'll see something like Figure 16.2.

Figure 16.2 Metadata Description

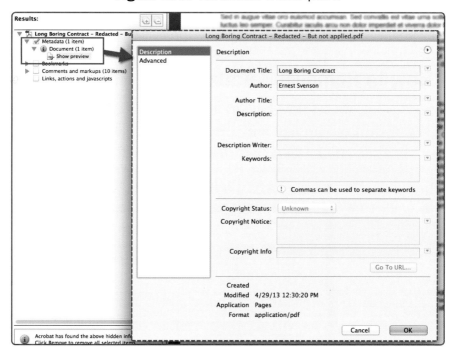

Description is the default (and you can see this document contains nothing really harmful, which is usually the case). You can select **Advanced** for more information, but don't expect to find anything horrific there, either. Even though the odds are that most PDFs won't have any incriminating metadata, you should make it a practice to run this feature before sending documents to opposing counsel or to anyone who might try to analyze the document to uncover hidden information.

16.2 How to Sanitize a Document

Another option is to "sanitize" the document (***Tools > Protection > Sanitize Document***), which does an even more thorough cleaning, as shown by the dialog box in Figure 16.3.

You may not use the Remove Hidden Information and Sanitize Document options very often, but you should at least know what they do and how they work. The best way to find out is to experiment, using them once in awhile even if you don't really need to.

Figure 16.3 Sanitize Document

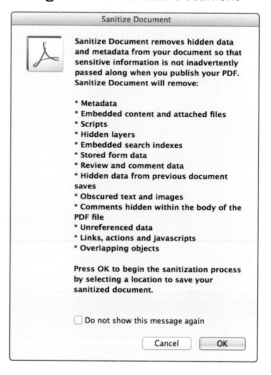

Sanitize Document

Sanitize Document removes hidden data and metadata from your document so that sensitive information is not inadvertently passed along when you publish your PDF. Sanitize Document will remove:

* Metadata
* Embedded content and attached files
* Scripts
* Hidden layers
* Embedded search indexes
* Stored form data
* Review and comment data
* Hidden data from previous document saves
* Obscured text and images
* Comments hidden within the body of the PDF file
* Unreferenced data
* Links, actions and javascripts
* Overlapping objects

Press OK to begin the sanitization process by selecting a location to save your sanitized document.

☐ Do not show this message again

Cancel   OK

Section 17

Find and Advanced Search

We've talked a lot about text-searchable PDFs, and how to make PDFs text searchable. Now it's time to talk about how to search for text within PDFs.

17.1 Finding Text

If you want to run a search on a PDF, open the *Edit* menu, and you'll find two options: **Find** and **Advanced Search**. It would behoove you to memorize the shortcut for using Find (**CMD/CTRL + F**), since you'll probably be using it a lot. If you try to run a **Find** search on a document that isn't text searchable, you'll get a warning dialog box, in which case you should refer back to Section 11.

Once you select the Find command, whether by menu choice or keyboard shortcut, you'll notice that a search box appears in the upper right-hand portion of Acrobat's interface, just below the Task Panes.

Figure 17.1 Using the Find Command

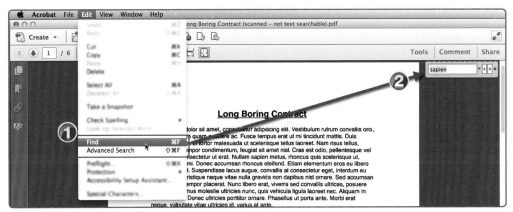

Type in the word or words you want to search on and hit ***Enter***. Acrobat will highlight the first instance of the search term in blue. Keep hitting Enter to move to each place the search term appears (you can also click on the little left or right arrows next to the search box, but that's less efficient).

If you want more options for how the search is performed, you can open a small drop-down menu in the search box, as shown in Figure 17.2.

Figure 17.2 Options for Find Command

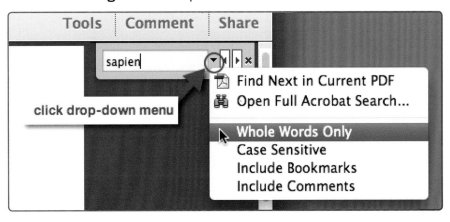

You can search on whole words or make your search case sensitive. You can also include bookmarks and comments in your search. Choosing **Open Full Acrobat Search** will trigger the Advanced Search feature that you saw on the Edit menu in Figure 17.1. (Why didn't Adobe just call it "Advanced Find"?).

You can keep hitting the Enter key to move to the next search term, but what if you want to move back one term? The official keyboard shortcut for moving forward from search term to search term is **CMD/CTRL + G**, and for moving back it's **CMD/CTRL + Shift + G**. It's easy to remember to hit **Enter** to keep moving forward, but you'll have to remember the shortcut if you want to move back and forth.

17.2 Advanced Search

If you choose Advanced Search instead of Find, you'll see a search dialog box open on the left-hand side of the document (see Figure 17.3). Many of the same options you were able to access from the drop-down menu under the Task Pane are available here as well. But you'll also be given the choice to search within PDF files other than the one in which you're currently working.

Figure 17.3 Advanced Search

The dialog box on the left is actually a floating window that you can move around as you see fit. The search box here is larger than the one for Find, but it is limited in the same way: no Boolean operators (i.e., *and*, *not*, *or*) are allowed. Once you choose the locations where you want the search performed, click the ***Search*** button. Then you'll see results something like Figure 17.4.

Figure 17.4 Results from Advanced Search

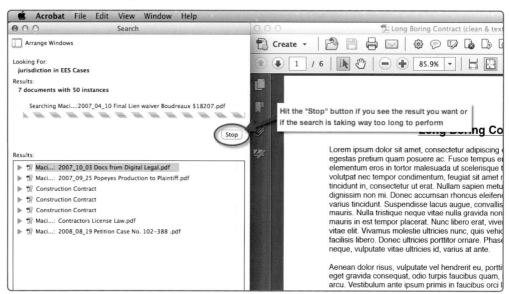

You can hit the ***Stop*** button if you see the search result you want or if the search is taking too long. For example, I started a search for the word *jurisdiction* in all of the PDFs in my open case files, and Acrobat took ten minutes to find 124 documents, containing 1,656 instances of that word. How much longer it would have taken to find them all? I don't know, because I hit the Stop button.

Once you hit Stop, you'll have to start the search from scratch if you want to look for those same terms again. You can save the search results you've collected by clicking on the little disk icon (circled in Figure 17.5) that appears when the search is finished (or when you stop it).

Figure 17.5 Save Search Results

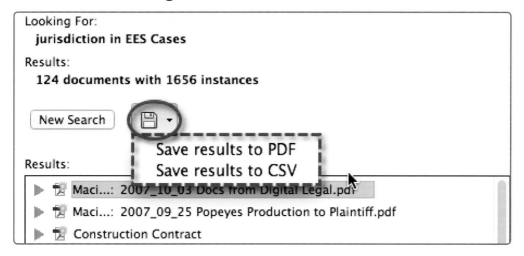

The results can be saved to a PDF, in which case Acrobat will create a hyperlinked PDF document that you can use to analyze search results. You can also save to a CSV file, which is best if you want to use a spreadsheet-type program to keep track of the results.

17.3 Search Indexes

If you want to search across a particular PDF data set with some regularity, you should create a search index (an Acrobat Pro feature only). To do this, open the ***Tools*** menu and look for **Document Processing**. There's a good chance you won't find it listed, as is the case in the screenshot shown in Figure 17.6.

Figure 17.6
Create Search Index

Figure 17.7 Enable Document Processing Panel

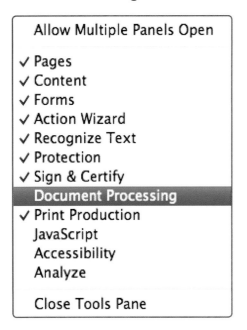

Figure 17.8 Choose Full Text with Catalogue

If you click in the little ***Options*** menu (see red circle), you'll get a list of all the possible task tools, some of which may be hidden (unchecked). Click ***Document Processing*** to select it, and then you'll be able to see it in your Tools menu (see Figure 17.7).

Now you're ready and able to create a search index. Under ***Document Processing***, choose ***Full Text Index with Catalog***, as shown in Figure 17.8.

Then the **Catalog** dialog box will appear to help you build your index: (1) click ***New Index***, (2) enter the index title and description, (3) designate which directories to include (and any to exclude), and then (4) click ***Build***.

Figure 17.9 Build Index

Acrobat will build a search index, which you can later open and rebuild if you have new documents that need to be included. To use the index, open the Advanced Search option (***Edit > Advanced Search***) and then choose ***Show More Options*** from the bottom. Then, back up at the top of the Advanced Search pane, you'll see a **Look In:** option. From there, select the index you created, as shown in Figure 17.10.

Figure 17.10

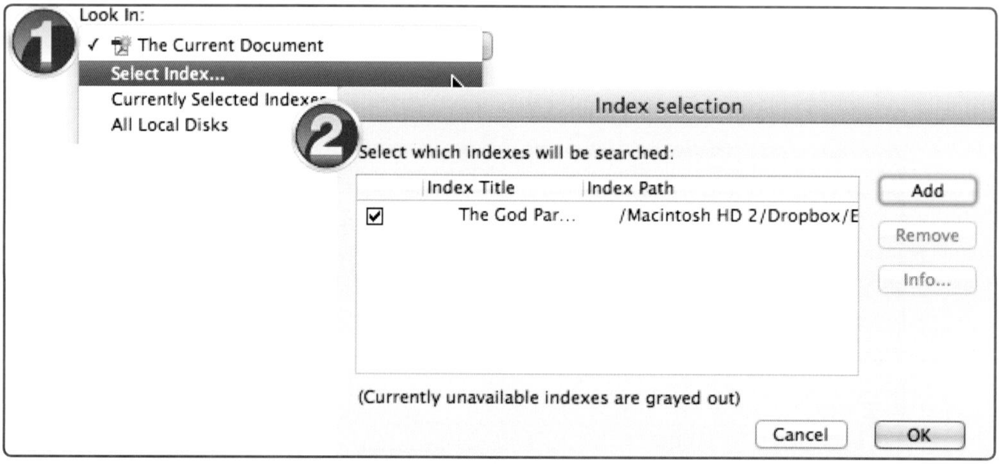

Now you'll be able to search PDFs using the index that you created, which will be much faster than doing a general search across a batch of files. Obviously, building an index takes time, so it won't be worth it in many instances. But if you are running a lot of searches in a certain set of folders, this is something you'll want to do.

Caveat: if you've created searchable PDFs using the OCR function described in Section 11, remember that OCR isn't perfect; you can't depend on it as a fail-safe method. If you need highly reliable searching of case documents, then you should consider a more sophisticated e-discovery review tool designed for complex cases.

PDF Security

PDF files are potentially more secure than paper documents, at least if you apply security to them. PDF security isn't infallible, but it's important for lawyers to know how to enable it, and to know what it can and can't do.

18.1 Two Types of Security

Acrobat allows you to lock down PDF files in two ways: (1) to prevent a user from opening a PDF without a "document open password," and (2) to restrict what can be done to a PDF once opened, unless the user enters a "document permissions password."

Why would you want to restrict PDFs in these ways? The answer no doubt varies from lawyer to lawyer, but here are some common scenarios.

Let's say you want to send a confidential document to a client by e-mail, but you're wary that a spouse or secretary might have access to the client's e-mail program. You should enable security that prevents the PDF from being opened without a password; then call your client and tell him or her the password (and perhaps keep that password for any future PDFs you need to send to that client).

If you're producing documents in PDF form to opposing counsel, you might want to restrict their ability to insert or remove pages. If the PDFs are text searchable, you might want to inhibit the ability to select and copy text (although doing so would likely create problems under F.R.C.P. 34(b)(E)(ii), which requires that documents be produced in a "reasonably usable form"). If a protective order specifies that the documents are not to be printed out, you could properly restrict printing.

18.2 Setting Security

So, how do you enable security to accomplish such goals? From the *File* menu, choose *Document Properties* (or use the shortcut **CMD/CTRL + D**) and click on the *Security* tab. From there, choose the *Security Method* drop-down menu (see Figure 18.1).

Figure 18.1 Enable Document Security

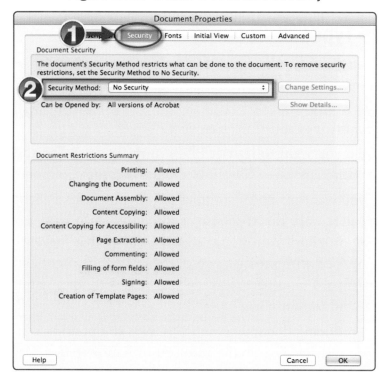

Choose **Password Security** from the drop-down, as shown in Figure 18.2.

From the next dialog box, you can (1) enter a password that will be needed to open the PDF, (2) enter a password that will be needed to make changes to the PDF, and (3) specify the changes that are allowed or disallowed.

Figure 18.2 Choose Password Security

Figure 18.3 Security Options

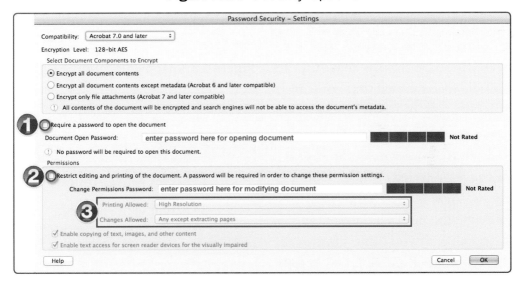

As you can see in Figure 18.3, you have options to prohibit printing (or limit printing quality) and restrict changes (e.g., inserting or deleting pages, content copying, and commenting). You can also set a password to restrict modifications to a PDF without setting a password for opening it.

18.3 PDF Security Isn't Perfect

After you apply security, Adobe will warn you that, while all of its products will enforce security settings, some third-party products might not, enabling recipients of your secured PDF to bypass some of the restrictions you set. In other words, Acrobat's security is pretty good, but far from perfect. Still, it's better than nothing, and therefore useful.

18.4 Save Security Settings for Reuse

If you find that you benefit from using the security settings, you might start using them a lot. And you might notice that you're using a certain set of security restrictions over and over. The good news is that you can create a saved policy that you can quickly apply to future PDFs.

Figure 18.4 Apply Security Settings

To do this, go to the *Tools* menu and select *Protection > Encrypt > Manage Security Policies*. Then, choose *New > Use Passwords* and give the policy a name (and description, if you like). From there, you'll see a dialog box exactly like the one in Figure 18.4, and you can define the security settings you want to save for future use.

When you want to apply the saved security settings, open the *Tools* menu and select *Protection > Encrypt*. Choose the policy you created and apply it to the open document.

The last important thing to mention about security is that you should regularly update Acrobat (and Reader, if you use that too). Adobe is always pushing out important security patches, and you want to have those as soon as they are available. To check for updates go to ***Help > Check for Updates***.

PDF/A

PDF/A is a widely recognized subset of the PDF standard designed for long term archiving. Since the primary goal of PDF/A is long-term archiving, it excludes those PDF features that would hamper access to the file later on. For more information on PDF/A, read this article from the University of Michigan: http://is.gd/qg4CcH

19.1 Why All the Fuss about PDF/As?

Federal courts are moving toward adopting PDF/A as the standard format for electronic filing. Why transition to PDF/A? Basically, to ensure that electronic records are preserved as far into the future as possible, in compliance with the requirements of the National Archives and Records Administration.

Federal courts will vary as to when they start requiring that documents be filed in the PDF/A format, but all courts currently will accept PDF/A files if they are uploaded to the CM/ECF system.

One key aspect of PDF/A is that it doesn't have all the features of a regular PDF. For example, multimedia files are disabled, so an embedded audio or video file would not work. Hyperlinks are also not preserved, at least not "masked hyperlinks." A string of text such as <u>Click here</u>, which clearly contains a link, is a masked hyperlink. An unmasked hyperlink would look like this: <u>http://www.pdfforlawyers.com</u>. Supposedly, unmasked hyperlinks might still work in a PDF/A document. But some tests suggest that they do not.

Why should lawyers care about whether links (masked or unmasked) work in PDF/A format?

Well, increasingly, lawyers are discovering that having the ability to link to external material is a useful tool. One could easily imagine a brief where each case citation was a hyperlink to the case in Google Advanced Scholar. Or, if a lawyer needed to cite to a video deposition that was stored on YouTube, he or she could connect to the deposition using a hyperlink. PDF/A almost certainly won't allow these kinds of actions.

Be prepared for misinformation from vendors wanting to make you think you need to buy something new to deal with PDF/A. Ignore anyone who says that lawyers will need to figure out how to mass-convert their current PDFs to PDF/A. Lawyers won't need to do that because the federal courts' requirement will kick in on a going-forward basis. New filings will, at some point, have to be made in PDF/A format, but the old stuff is in the system, and no one is going to expect lawyers to refile all their pleadings.

19.2 How to Create a PDF/A

Creating a PDF/A from an existing PDF is easy, but the choices have slightly different names in Acrobat X versus Acrobat XI. Here's the process for each version of Acrobat.

In Acrobat X, choose:

1. *File*
2. *Save As*
3. *More Options*
4. *PDF/A*

In Acrobat XI, choose:

1. *File*
2. *Save As Other*
3. *Archivable PDF (PDF/A)*

Appendix

Recommended Preference Settings

I recommended several preference settings in Section 1, but here they are again in a simple checklist format. To access the Preferences dialog box on a PC select **Edit > Preferences**. On a Mac select **Adobe > Preferences**.

Commenting

☐ Enable "Copy selected text into highlight, strikethrough, and underline comment pop-ups."

Documents

☐ Review "Documents in recently used list" to see if you want to change it to more docs

☐ Review **Redaction** to see if you like the default suffix ("_Redacted")

General

- ☐ Enable "Use single-key accelerators to access tools."
- ☐ Review **Messages from Adobe** to see if you want messages upon launch.
- ☐ Review **Application Startup** and disable "Show welcome screen" if it annoys you.

Page Display

- ☐ Review **Page Layout** and **Zoom** settings, and adjust to your preferences (but remember that specific settings in a PDF will override your application settings).

Identity

- ☐ Review your identity information, and fill out the fields that make sense for you.

E-mail Accounts (Acrobat XI only)

- ☐ Review and add any accounts from which you want to allow Acrobat to send e-mail (Acrobat XI now supports Gmail and Yahoo! e-mail accounts).

Updater

- ☐ Choose if you want Acrobat to automatically download updates

Keyboard Shortcut Cheat Sheet

 **Control - PC**    **Command - Mac**

—Use the appropriate keyboard modifier, depending on what kind of computer you use—

Document Review: <u>Cntrl/Cmd</u> + **D**

- File Size, number of pages
- Security: problems with doc? Check permissions to see if something is not allowed.
- Initial view: set to show bookmarks, or attachments, if PDF has those.

Zoom: <u>Cntrl/Cmd</u> + **Plus or Minus**

- Use **+** to zoom in, and use **–** to zoom out
- Hold **Spacebar** while dragging to move around in zoomed view

Page View: <u>Cntrl/Cmd</u> + **0** (for 'Fit Page')

  <u>Cntrl/Cmd</u> + **2** (for 'Fit Width')

Jump to Page: <u>Cntrl/Cmd</u> + **SHIFT + N** (then enter page #)

Back to Prior View: <u>Cmd/Cntrl</u> + **LEFT ARROW** (←)

Rotate Page: <u>Cntrl/Cmd</u> + **SHIFT + Plus or Minus** (rotates all pages, left or right)

Rotate Pages: <u>Cmd/Cntrl</u> + **SHIFT + R** (calls up dialogue box with options)

Bookmarking: <u>Cntrl/Cmd</u> + **B**

- Or <u>select text first</u>, and <u>then hit keyboard shortcut</u> to make bookmark name same as text (if you can't select text then you need to make the text searchable via **Recognize Text** option

Commenting (pop up bubble): <u>Cntrl/Cmd</u> + **6**

- After entering the desired text, hit **ESCAPE** key.

Find Text: <u>Cntrl/Cmd</u> + **F**

- Use + to zoom in, and use – to zoom out

Single Key Accelerators Cheat Sheet

To use these single-key accelerators, you have to enable them. First, go to the *Edit* menu and select *Preferences.* Second, in the *Categories Pane,* choose *General* and click the box next to the accelerators command, as shown.

Then, you can switch quickly between tools using these single key shortcuts.

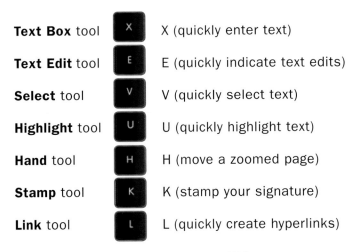

Text Box tool   X (quickly enter text)

Text Edit tool   E (quickly indicate text edits)

Select tool   V (quickly select text)

Highlight tool   U (quickly highlight text)

Hand tool   H (move a zoomed page)

Stamp tool   K (stamp your signature)

Link tool   L (quickly create hyperlinks)

Acrobat Pro v. Standard Checklist

There aren't too many differences between Acrobat Standard and Acrobat Professional (and remember, on the Mac there is only Professional). But here are some of the key functions that legal professionals will care about in each version.

Acrobat Standard Features (Professional has all of these)

- ☐ OCR or (Recognize Text)
- ☐ Text editing
- ☐ Form filling and saving
- ☐ Save to PDF/A

Acrobat Pro (these are not available in Standard)

- ☐ Bates stamping
- ☐ Redaction
- ☐ Actions (e.g., flattening)
- ☐ Plug-ins (e.g., AutoBookmark or Casemap)
- ☐ Embed video (if a case has video evidence and you want to produce it in PDF)

Adobe Reader:
Features and Limitations

With Adobe Reader you *cannot:*

- open non-PDF files (so, you can't import a PNG file to have a transparent signature)
- enable "copy selected text into comment field" as a preference
- edit text
- create bookmarks, or edit them
- set single key accelerators
- rearrange pages (you can do this on Mac with Preview)
- set "Initial View" to open with bookmarks
- export to Word or Excel (but you can pay $19.99/year for an export service from Adobe)
- merge files into PDF (but you can pay $9.99/month for the online CreatePDF program, or $75/year for unlimited merges)

With Adobe Reader you *can:*

- use all the keyboard shortcuts I put in the Keyboard Shortcut Cheat Sheet
- import a custom stamp, so you can have a signature (but it will have a white background)
- create highlights and comments
- change highlight color in properties

- globally change the author name to "liability" or other "tag" you want to use
- attach a file, but it has to have an icon and appear on a page (not in a separate panel)
- search inside a file attachment
- do Advanced Search

PDF Workflows in the Law Office

Legal Research

Since you aren't going to *edit* the cases you download from Lexis, Westlaw, FastCase, or CaseMaker, you should obtain those cases or statutes in PDF format. Then you simply need to organize them so you can make highlights and comments and get the most out of that valuable work product. Here's a useful workflow to accomplish that.

☐ Combine all legal research documents into one PDF (Section 5.7), or group them into separate PDFs according to different legal issues.

☐ If needed, you can rename the bookmarks that result when you combine the PDFs (Section 8.5), although in most cases the filenames will be the name of the case.

☐ Highlight key passages (Section 9.1), and make sticky note comments (Section 9.5).

☐ Create check boxes in the Comments List if you need to remember to review key passages or use them for quotes (this feature of the Comment List was discussed in Section 15.2 on Redaction Review).

☐ Change the author name to an issue code (if you want) by renaming the author in the Comment properties. You can do this in bulk if you want by opening the Comments List and selecting the comments with properties you want to change, then right-clicking and selecting Properties and making your desired changes.

End of Matter: Archive E-mails to PDF

In Section 5.11, we talked about how you can archive e-mails to PDF if you have the Windows version of Acrobat, and if you use Microsoft Outlook or Lotus notes for your e-mail program.

With Acrobat, you can archive e-mails one at a time or several at a time. You have to manually select each e-mail you want to archive by clicking on it and holding down either the Control key (PC) or the Command key (Mac).

You can also archive an entire folder of e-mails that you have set up in Microsoft Outlook or Lotus Notes. Obviously, this is most useful if you've been diligent about putting all e-mails related to a matter in a folder. If you've done that, then at the end of the matter you can archive all of those e-mails to PDF and save them to the case folder. That way, you'll always have access to the e-mails, even if you switch to a new e-mail program.

More Workflows

If you've developed some useful PDF workflows, send me an e-mail so I can share them via my PDFforLawyers.com weblog. And sign up for my e-mail newsletter to get the latest batch automatically. My email address is: ernie@paperlesschase.com.

Index

LinkedIn in One Hour for Lawyers, Second Edition
By Dennis Kennedy and Allison C. Shields

Product Code: 5110773 • LPM Price: $39.95 • Regular Price: $49.95

Since the first edition of LinkedIn in One Hour for Lawyers was published, LinkedIn has added almost 100 million users, and more and more lawyers are using the platform on a regular basis. Now, this bestselling ABA book has been fully revised and updated to reflect significant changes to LinkedIn's layout and functionality made through 2013. LinkedIn in One Hour for Lawyers, Second Edition, will help lawyers make the most of their online professional networking. In just one hour, you will learn to:

- Set up a LinkedIn® account
- Create a robust, dynamic profile--and take advantage of new multimedia options
- Build your connections
- Get up to speed on new features such as Endorsements, Influencers, Contacts, and Channels
- Enhance your Company Page with new functionality
- Use search tools to enhance your network
- Monitor your network with ease
- Optimize your settings for privacy concerns
- Use LinkedIn® effectively in the hiring process
- Develop a LinkedIn strategy to grow your legal network

Blogging in One Hour for Lawyers
By Ernie Svenson

Product Code: 5110744 • LPM Price: $24.95 • Regular Price: $39.95

Until a few years ago, only the largest firms could afford to engage an audience of millions. Now, lawyers in any size firm can reach a global audience at little to no cost—all because of blogs. An effective blog can help you promote your practice, become more "findable" online, and take charge of how you are perceived by clients, journalists and anyone who uses the Internet. Blogging in One Hour for Lawyers will show you how to create, maintain, and improve a legal blog—and gain new business opportunities along the way. In just one hour, you will learn to:

- Set up a blog quickly and easily
- Write blog posts that will attract clients
- Choose from various hosting options like Blogger, TypePad, and WordPress
- Make your blog friendly to search engines, increasing your ranking
- Tweak the design of your blog by adding customized banners and colors
- Easily send notice of your blog posts to Facebook and Twitter
- Monitor your blog's traffic with Google Analytics and other tools
- Avoid ethics problems that may result from having a legal blog

The Electronic Evidence and Discovery Handbook: Forms, Checklists, and Guidelines
By Sharon D. Nelson, Bruce A. Olson, and John W. Simek

Product Code: 5110569 • LPM Price: $99.95 • Regular Price: $129.95

The use of electronic evidence has increased dramatically over the past few years, but many lawyers still struggle with the complexities of electronic discovery. This substantial book provides lawyers with the templates they need to frame their discovery requests and provides helpful advice on what they can subpoena. In addition to the ready-made forms, the authors also supply explanations to bring you up to speed on the electronic discovery field. The accompanying CD-ROM features over 70 forms, including, Motions for Protective Orders, Preservation and Spoliation Documents, Motions to Compel, Electronic Evidence Protocol Agreements, Requests for Production, Internet Services Agreements, and more. Also included is a full electronic evidence case digest with over 300 cases detailed!

Facebook® in One Hour for Lawyers
By Dennis Kennedy and Allison C. Shields

Product Code: 5110745 • LPM Price: $24.95 • Regular Price: $39.95

With a few simple steps, lawyers can use Facebook® to market their services, grow their practices, and expand their legal network—all by using the same methods they already use to communicate with friends and family. Facebook® in One Hour for Lawyers will show any attorney—from Facebook® novices to advanced users—how to use this powerful tool for both professional and personal purposes.

Android Apps in One Hour for Lawyers
By Daniel J. Siegel

Product Code: 5110754 • LPM Price: $19.95 • Regular Price: $34.95

Lawyers are already using Android devices to make phone calls, check e-mail, and send text messages. After the addition of several key apps, Android smartphones or tablets can also help run a law practice. From the more than 800,000 apps currently available, Android Apps in One Hour for Lawyers highlights the "best of the best" apps that will allow you to practice law from your mobile device. In just one hour, this book will describe how to buy, install, and update Android apps, and help you:

- Store documents and files in the cloud
- Use security apps to safeguard client data on your phone
- Be organized and productive with apps for to-do lists, calendar, and contacts
- Communicate effectively with calling, text, and e-mail apps
- Create, edit, and organize your documents
- Learn on the go with news, reading, and reference apps
- Download utilities to keep your device running smoothly
- Hit the road with apps for travel
- Have fun with games and social media apps

Virtual Law Practice:
How to Deliver Legal Services Online
By Stephanie L. Kimbro

Product Code: 5110707 • LPM Price: $47.95 • Regular Price: $79.95

The legal market has recently experienced a dramatic shift as lawyers seek out alternative methods of practicing law and providing more affordable legal services. Virtual law practice is revolutionizing the way the public receives legal services and how legal professionals work with clients. If you are interested in this form of practicing law, *Virtual Law Practice* will help you:

- Responsibly deliver legal services online to your clients
- Successfully set up and operate a virtual law office
- Establish a virtual law practice online through a secure, client-specific portal
- Manage and market your virtual law practice
- Understand state ethics and advisory opinions
- Find more flexibility and work/life balance in the legal profession

Social Media for Lawyers: The Next Frontier
By Carolyn Elefant and Nicole Black

Product Code: 5110710 • LPM Price: $47.95 • Regular Price: $79.95

The world of legal marketing has changed with the rise of social media sites such as Linkedin, Twitter, and Facebook. Law firms are seeking their companies attention with tweets, videos, blog posts, pictures, and online content. Social media is fast and delivers news at record pace. This book provides you with a practical, goal-centric approach to using social media in your law practice that will enable you to identify social media platforms and tools that fit your practice and implement them easily, efficiently, and ethically.

iPad Apps in One Hour for Lawyers
By Tom Mighell

Product Code: 5110739 • LPM Price: $19.95 • Regular Price: $34.95

At last count, there were more than 80,000 apps available for the iPad. Finding the best apps often can be an overwhelming, confusing, and frustrating process. iPad Apps in One Hour for Lawyers provides the "best of the best" apps that are essential for any law practice. In just one hour, you will learn about the apps most worthy of your time and attention. This book will describe how to buy, install, and update iPad apps, and help you:

- Find apps to get organized and improve your productivity
- Create, manage, and store documents on your iPad
- Choose the best apps for your law office, including litigation and billing apps
- Find the best news, reading, and reference apps
- Take your iPad on the road with apps for travelers
- Maximize your social networking power
- Have some fun with game and entertainment apps during your relaxation time

Twitter in One Hour for Lawyers
By Jared Correia

Product Code: 5110746 • LPM Price: $24.95 • Regular Price: $39.95

More lawyers than ever before are using Twitter to network with colleagues, attract clients, market their law firms, and even read the news. But to the uninitiated, Twitter's short messages, or tweets, can seem like they are written in a foreign language. Twitter in One Hour for Lawyers will demystify one of the most important social-media platforms of our time and teach you to tweet like an expert. In just one hour, you will learn to.

- Create a Twitter account and set up your profile
- Read tweets and understand Twitter jargon
- Write tweets—and send them at the appropriate time
- Gain an audience—follow and be followed
- Engage with other Twitters users
- Integrate Twitter into your firm's marketing plan
- Cross-post your tweets with other social media platforms like Facebook and LinkedIn
- Understand the relevant ethics, privacy, and security concerns
- Get the greatest possible return on your Twitter investment
- And much more!

The Lawyer's Essential Guide to Writing
By Marie Buckley

Product Code: 5110726 • LPM Price: $47.95 • Regular Price: $79.95

This is a readable, concrete guide to contemporary legal writing. Based on Marie Buckley's years of experience coaching lawyers, this book provides a systematic approach to all forms of written communication, from memoranda and briefs to e-mail and blogs. The book sets forth three principles for powerful writing and shows how to apply those principles to develop a clean and confident style.

iPad in One Hour for Lawyers, Second Edition
By Tom Mighell

Product Code: 5110747 • LPM Price: $24.95 • Regular Price: $39.95

Whether you are a new or a more advanced iPad user, *iPad in One Hour for Lawyers* takes a great deal of the mystery and confusion out of using your iPad. Ideal for lawyers who want to get up to speed swiftly, this book presents the essentials so you don't get bogged down in technical jargon and extraneous features and apps. In just six, short lessons, you'll learn how to:

- Quickly Navigate and Use the iPad User Interface
- Set Up Mail, Calendar, and Contacts
- Create and Use Folders to Multitask and Manage Apps
- Add Files to Your iPad, and Sync Them
- View and Manage Pleadings, Case Law, Contracts, and other Legal Documents
- Use Your iPad to Take Notes and Create Documents
- Use Legal-Specific Apps at Trial or in Doing Research

30-DAY RISK-FREE ORDER FORM

ABA LAW PRACTICE DIVISION
The Business of Practicing Law

Please print or type. To ship UPS, we must have your street address. If you list a P.O. Box, we will ship by U.S. Mail.

Name

Member ID

Firm/Organization

Street Address

City/State/Zip

Area Code/Phone (In case we have a question about your order)

E-mail

Method of Payment:
☐ Check enclosed, payable to American Bar Association
☐ MasterCard   ☐ Visa   ☐ American Express

Card Number   Expiration Date

Signature Required

MAIL THIS FORM TO:
American Bar Association, Publication Orders
P.O. Box 10892, Chicago, IL 60610

ORDER BY PHONE:
24 hours a day, 7 days a week:
Call 1-800-285-2221 to place a credit card order. We accept Visa, MasterCard, and American Express.

EMAIL ORDERS: orders@americanbar.org
FAX ORDERS: 1-312-988-5568

VISIT OUR WEB SITE: www.ShopABA.org
Allow 7-10 days for regular UPS delivery. Need it sooner? Ask about our overnight delivery options. Call the ABA Service Center at 1-800-285-2221 for more information.

GUARANTEE:
If–for any reason–you are not satisfied with your purchase, you may return it within 30 days of receipt for a refund of the price of the book(s). No questions asked.

Thank You For Your Order.

Join the ABA Law Practice Division today and receive a substantial discount on Division publications!

Product Code:	Description:	Quantity:	Price:	Total Price:
				$
				$
				$
				$
				$

Shipping/Handling:		*Tax:		
$0.00 to $9.99	add $0.00	IL residents add 9.25% DC residents add 6%	Subtotal:	$
$10.00 to $49.99	add $5.95		*Tax:	$
$50.00 to $99.99	add $7.95		**Shipping/Handling:	$
$100.00 to $199.99	add $9.95	Yes, I am an ABA member and would like to join the Law Practice Division today! (Add $50.00)		$
$200.00 to $499.99	add $12.95		Total:	$